party
food

party
food

Great recipes for
quick and delicious
party food

Jan Stephenson

This is a Parragon Publishing Book
This edition published in 2006

Parragon Publishing
Queen Street House
4 Queen Street
Bath BA1 1HE
United Kingdom

ISBN: 1-40547-248-0
Printed in China

Designed and produced by
THE BRIDGEWATER BOOK COMPANY

Cover by Talking Design

Notes for the Reader:

This book uses imperial, metric, and US
cup measurements. Follow the same
units of measurement throughout; do
not mix imperial and metric. All spoon
measurements are level: teaspoons are
assumed to be 5 ml, and tablespoons
are assumed to be 15 ml. Unless
otherwise stated, milk is assumed
to be whole, eggs and individual
vegetables such as potatoes are
medium, and pepper is freshly ground
black pepper.

Recipes using raw or very lightly cooked
eggs should be avoided by infants, the
elderly, pregnant women, convalescents,
and anyone suffering from an illness.
The times given are an approximate
guide only, and may vary according to
the techniques and equipment used by
different people.

CONTENTS

INTRODUCTION

There's always a good reason to throw a party—it's your birthday, you've got a new job, you've moved into a bigger place, it's Friday night—and there are party styles in this book to match every kind of celebration and every season of the year.

Whatever the size of the party you're planning, effortless entertaining is the keynote to all the recipes—it's no fun feeling like a limp rag by the time your guests arrive. There are lots of ideas for preparing food in advance—even hot snacks can often be oven-ready well before the doorbell rings.

If you're in the mood for a bit of glamor, turn to Canapé and Cocktail Chic for an array of stylish snacks, nibbles, pâtés, and dips, from the cool-tasting Tzatziki (see page 35) to the delectable Olive & Tomato Bruschetta (see page 37), designed to counterbalance the effects of over a dozen classic cocktails and variations that round off the chapter. If the weather is looking good and you fancy some alfresco entertaining, check out chapter two for some sizzling barbecue dishes, salads, and other recipes, including old friends like Hamburgers (see

page 69), all complemented by some desserts and drinks such as Homemade Lemonade (see page 80). When winter drives you indoors but you're still driven to put on a party, turn to chapter three for more substantial warming recipes and Christmas treats. Spontaneous party people will find Fast Fun Fare invaluable—there are some quick and easy to prepare recipes, from the Speedy Chili Beef (see page 129) to Tomato & Mozzarella Pizzas (see page 128), that can be the focal point of the evening or a quick snack if you fancy a T.V. party. Finally, for those who love to entertain but find dinner parties just a bit too old-fashioned and stuffy, Super Supper Parties provides the answer with a tantalizing assortment of easy-cook international dishes that are meals in themselves.

Don't forget all the important extras and accessories—ice cubes, supply of plates, glasses, and cutlery, and lots of table napkins. None of the recipes requires any special kitchen equipment although you may find a measure and a shaker useful if you intend to serve cocktails. Getting the proportions right is the secret of successful mixed drinks and a standard measure avoids complicated mental arithmetic. Now go and enjoy your party!

CANAPÉ &
COCKTAIL
CHIC

4 boneless pork steaks or
4 skinless, boneless
chicken breasts

vegetable oil, for brushing

fresh cilantro sprigs, to garnish

freshly cooked rice, to serve

Marinade

2 tbsp finely chopped onion

1 garlic clove, finely chopped

2 tbsp chopped fresh cilantro

2 tbsp soy sauce

¼ tsp ground ginger

¼ tsp sugar

1 tbsp vegetable oil

Peanut sauce

1 small onion, finely chopped

2 garlic cloves, finely chopped

1 fresh red chili, seeded and
finely chopped

1 tbsp brown sugar

1 tbsp vegetable oil

generous ⅜ cup crunchy
peanut butter

1 tbsp lemon or lime juice

1 tbsp dark soy sauce

1¾ cups coconut milk

SATAY STICKS

Cut the meat into thin slices, about 2 inches/5 cm long. Combine the marinade ingredients in a shallow dish. Add the meat and stir well. Cover with plastic wrap and let chill for 1–2 hours.

For the sauce, blend the onion, garlic, chili, and sugar into a coarse paste in a food processor. Cook in the oil in a small pan over medium heat for 5 minutes. Add the remaining sauce ingredients and mix well. Bring to a boil, then let simmer, stirring constantly, for 15 minutes, or until slightly thickened.

Preheat a stove-top grill pan over high heat. Meanwhile, drain the meat and thread onto skewers that will fit comfortably on the grill pan. Brush with oil and cook on the grill pan for 3–4 minutes on each side, or until the meat is cooked right through.

Serve the satay sticks on a bed of rice, garnished with cilantro. Place the peanut sauce in a small serving dish as an accompaniment.

SERVES 4

generous ¾ cup white bread flour, plus extra for dusting

½ tsp active dry yeast

½ tsp salt

1 tbsp olive oil

½–1 cup warm water

Topping

4 tbsp olive oil

1 large onion, thinly sliced

1 tsp brown sugar

1 tsp balsamic vinegar

2 oz/55 g feta, mozzarella, or Gorgonzola cheese, grated or sliced

Mix the flour, yeast, and salt together in a bowl. Drizzle over half the oil. Make a well in the flour and pour in the water. Mix to a firm ball of dough. Turn out onto a floured counter and knead until it is no longer sticky. Add more flour if necessary. Oil the bowl with the remaining oil. Return the dough to the bowl and turn once to coat. Cover with a clean dish towel and let rise for 1 hour in a warm place.

Heat the oil for the topping in a pan over medium heat. Add the onion and cook for 10 minutes. Sprinkle with the sugar and cook for an additional 5 minutes, stirring occasionally. Add the vinegar and cook for an additional 5 minutes. Remove from the heat and let cool.

Preheat the oven to 425°F/220°C. When the dough has doubled in size, turn out and punch down to release excess air, then knead until smooth. Divide into quarters and roll out into thin circles. Place the dough circles on a baking sheet, spread with the cooked onion, and top with the cheese. Bake in the oven for 10 minutes. Remove from the oven and serve.

MINIATURE ONION PIZZAS

EGG ROLLS

Shell the eggs, cut in half lengthwise, and remove the yolks. Mash the yolks, or place in a food processor, with the tuna, 2 anchovies, 4 olives, and all the capers.

Blend the ingredients together to make a smooth paste, adding 1 teaspoon of the reserved oil from the anchovies, or some extra virgin olive oil, to achieve the correct consistency.

Arrange the egg whites on an attractive serving dish. Fill the hollows with the yolk mixture using either a teaspoon or a pastry bag. Make sure the filling is piled high.

Cut the remaining anchovies and olives into tiny strips and use them to garnish the filled eggs, then serve.

DEVILED EGGS

SERVES 4

8 hard-cooked eggs

2 tbsp drained canned tuna

4 anchovy fillets, canned or bottled in olive oil, drained and oil reserved (optional)

6 black olives, pitted

1 tsp capers, rinsed and drained

CRUNCHY POTATO SKINS

SERVES 4

4 large potatoes, cooked in
their skins

2 lean bacon slices

1 cup crumbled blue cheese

vegetable oil, for deep-frying

To garnish
sour cream
fresh chives

Preheat the broiler to high. Cut the potatoes into fourths and scoop out the flesh, leaving a lining about ¼ inch/5 mm thick.

Cook the bacon under the broiler until crisp. Transfer to a plate and cut into small strips. Combine the bacon with the cheese in a small bowl.

Heat the oil over a high heat in a deep pan or wok to 350–375°F/180–190°C, or until a cube of bread browns in 30 seconds. Carefully drop the potato skins into the oil and deep-fry for 3–4 minutes, or until crisp and golden. Remove and drain well on paper towels.

Arrange the potato skins on a large plate and fill each with a spoonful of the bacon and cheese mixture, piling it high so that it is almost overflowing. Garnish with a teaspoon of sour cream and chives and serve at once.

Preheat the oven to 400°F/200°C.

Brush the pita breads with oil and sprinkle with whichever toppings you have decided to use.

Arrange the bread on a baking sheet and cook in the oven for 5 minutes, or until crispy and golden. Remove from the oven, cut into fingers or triangles, and serve at once with a selection of dips and spreads (see pages 22–35).

SERVES 4

4 pita breads or bagels, cut into thin slices horizontally

2 tbsp olive oil or melted butter

Toppings

1 tsp black onion, dill, cumin, or crushed coriander seeds (optional)

1 tsp finely chopped fresh rosemary (optional)

1 tsp sea salt (optional)

2 garlic cloves, finely chopped (optional)

SPECIALTY BREAD CHIPS

CHEESE STRAWS

Preheat the oven to 400°F/200°C. Grease a baking sheet.

Sprinkle the counter with flour, then roll out the pastry to make a large rectangle.

Spread the mustard, cheese, and cayenne, if using, over the pastry, then cut it into thin strips about 4 inches/10 cm long.

Carefully lay the straws on the baking sheet, transfer to the oven, and bake for 10 minutes, or until crisp and golden.

Remove from the oven, let cool and then serve in baskets or piled high.

SERVES 4

vegetable oil or butter,
for greasing

all-purpose flour, for dusting

8 oz/225 g ready-made puff pastry,
thawed if frozen

1 tsp mustard (optional)

2 tbsp grated Cheddar cheese
a mixture of Cheddar and
Parmesan cheese

cayenne pepper (optional)

SPINACH, FETA & TOMATO TRIANGLES

HAM & PARMESAN PINWHEELS

Preheat the oven to 400°F/200°C. Grease a baking sheet.

Heat the oil in a pan over medium heat and cook the shallot for 2–3 minutes. Add the spinach, increase the heat to high, and cook, stirring constantly, for 2–3 minutes. Remove from the heat and drain. Chop coarsely, season to taste with salt and pepper, and let cool.

Cut each sheet of pastry into 6 strips. Place a spoonful of spinach at the bottom of each strip. Sprinkle cheese and tomatoes on top. Fold the bottom right-hand corner of each strip up to meet the opposite side to form a triangle. Fold the triangle toward the top of the strip and repeat until you reach the top of the strip.

Brush the edges of each triangle with melted butter, then transfer to the baking sheet. Brush the top of the triangles with more butter. Bake in the oven for 10 minutes, or until the pastry is golden and crispy. Remove from the oven and serve at once.

SERVES 4

2 tbsp olive oil

2 tbsp finely chopped shallot

2½ cups fresh spinach leaves, washed and shredded

2 sheets phyllo pastry

1 cup crumbled feta cheese (drained weight)

6 sun-dried tomatoes, finely chopped

4 oz/115 g butter, melted, plus extra for greasing

salt and pepper

SPINACH, FETA & TOMATO TRIANGLES

HAM & PARMESAN PINWHEELS

SERVES 4

butter, for greasing

1 small loaf bread

4 tbsp butter, mustard, or cream cheese

4 slices ham (plain, cured, or smoked)

4 tbsp freshly grated Parmesan cheese

8 sun-dried tomatoes (optional)

Preheat the oven to 350°F/180°C. Grease a baking sheet.

Remove the crusts from the bread and cut into 4 slices lengthwise. Place each slice between 2 pieces of waxed paper and flatten with a rolling pin. Remove the paper.

Spread each slice of bread with butter and top with slices of ham. Sprinkle Parmesan cheese over the top. If you are using sun-dried tomatoes, chop them and sprinkle over the cheese.

Roll up the bread along its length, then cut into ½-inch/1-cm slices crosswise. Place the pinwheels, cut-side up, on the baking sheet. Transfer to the oven and bake for 5 minutes, or until the cheese has melted. Remove from the oven, place on a dish, and serve either hot or cold.

CHICKEN & MIXED HERB PÂTÉ

SERVES 4

1 small mealy potato, diced

9 oz/250 g cooked skinless
chicken meat, diced

1 garlic clove, crushed

1 tbsp chopped fresh parsley

1 tbsp chopped fresh cilantro

½ tbsp grated lemon rind

2 tbsp lemon juice

generous ⅜ cup cream cheese

salt and pepper

sliced scallion, to garnish

To serve

pita breads, cut into triangles

vegetable crudités,
such as carrots and celery

lemon wedges

Cook the diced potato in a pan of lightly salted water for 10 minutes, or until tender, then drain well.

Transfer the potato to a food processor, then add the chicken, garlic, parsley, cilantro, lemon rind and juice, and salt and pepper to taste. Process until thoroughly blended. Alternatively, finely chop all the ingredients and mix together well.

Place the mixture in a large bowl and stir in the cream cheese. Cover with plastic wrap and let chill for 45 minutes.

Remove from the refrigerator and divide the pâté between individual serving dishes. Sprinkle over the sliced scallion to garnish and serve with pita bread triangles, vegetable crudités, and lemon wedges.

AÏOLI

Ensure that all the ingredients are at room temperature. Place the garlic and egg yolks in a food processor and process until well blended. With the motor running, pour in the oil, teaspoon by teaspoon, through the feeder tube until the mixture starts to thicken, then pour in the remaining oil in a thin stream until a thick mayonnaise forms.

Add the lemon and lime juices, mustard, and tarragon and season to taste with salt and pepper. Blend until smooth, then transfer to a nonmetallic bowl. Garnish with a tarragon sprig.

Cover with plastic wrap and let chill until required.

SERVES 4

3 large garlic cloves, finely chopped

2 egg yolks

1 cup extra virgin olive oil

1 tbsp lemon juice

1 tbsp lime juice

1 tbsp Dijon mustard

1 tbsp chopped fresh tarragon

salt and pepper

1 fresh tarragon sprig, to garnish

SESAME EGGPLANT DIP

Place the eggplant on a preheated stove-top grill pan or under a preheated broiler and cook, turning frequently, until the skin is black and blistered and the flesh is very soft.

Transfer to a cutting board and let cool slightly. Cut the eggplant in half and scoop out the flesh into a bowl. Mash with a fork to make a coarse paste.

Gradually add the oil, lemon juice, sesame seed paste, and garlic. Mix well, tasting until you achieve the flavor and texture you like.

Transfer the mixture to an attractive bowl and serve at room temperature. If not serving at once, cover with plastic wrap, and let chill until 30 minutes before required.

Just before serving, toss the sesame seeds in a very hot, dry skillet for a few seconds to toast them. Sprinkle over the eggplant dip to garnish.

SERVES 4

1 medium eggplant

4–6 tbsp olive oil

juice of 1–2 lemons

4–6 tbsp sesame seed paste

1–2 garlic cloves, crushed

1 tsp sesame seeds, to garnish

Cut the avocados in half, remove and discard the pits, and scoop the flesh into a large bowl. Mash to make a coarse paste.

Cut the tomato in half and remove and discard all the seeds. Dice the flesh and add to the avocados.

Stir in the lime juice to loosen the mixture slightly, then stir in the onion, cilantro, and chili, if using. Spoon into an attractive bowl, garnish with a cilantro sprig, and serve at once.

SERVES 4

2 ripe avocados

1 tomato

juice of 1 lime

1 tbsp finely chopped sweet onion

2 tbsp fresh cilantro, finely chopped

1 tbsp seeded and finely chopped fresh red or green chili (optional)

1 fresh cilantro sprig, to garnish

GUACAMOLE

TARAMASALATA

CRAB & CITRUS SALSA

SERVES 4

5½ oz/150 g skinless cod's roe

2 garlic cloves, finely chopped

2 shallots, finely chopped

6 tbsp lemon juice

1 tbsp finely grated lemon rind

4 slices fresh white bread, crusts removed

salt and pepper

½ cup olive oil

To garnish

1 lemon slice quarter

1 fresh flat-leaf parsley sprig

To serve

warmed pita breads

fresh salad greens

tomato slices

Place the cod's roe, garlic, shallots, and lemon juice and rind in a food processor and blend together well. Tear the bread into small pieces and add to the mixture. Season to taste with salt and pepper and blend until smooth.

With the motor running, gradually pour the oil through the feeder tube and blend until smooth. Transfer the mixture to a bowl, cover with plastic wrap, and let chill until required.

When ready to serve, garnish the taramasalata with a lemon slice quarter and a parsley sprig and serve with pita breads, salad greens, and tomato slices.

SERVES 4

9 oz/250 g canned or freshly cooked crabmeat

1 red bell pepper, seeded and chopped

4 tomatoes, chopped

3 scallions, chopped

1 tbsp chopped fresh flat-leaf parsley

1 fresh red chili, seeded and chopped

3 tbsp freshly squeezed lime juice

3 tbsp freshly squeezed orange juice

salt and pepper

To garnish
fresh flat-leaf parsley sprigs
lime wedges

To serve
carrots, cut into short thin sticks
celery stalks, cut into short thin sticks
tortilla chips

Drain the crabmeat, if using canned, and place in a large nonmetallic bowl with the bell pepper, tomatoes, scallions, parsley, and chili. Add the lime and orange juices, season to taste with salt and pepper, and mix well. Cover with plastic wrap and let chill for 30 minutes to allow the flavors to combine.

When ready to serve, remove the salsa from the refrigerator. Garnish with parsley sprigs and lime wedges and serve with carrot and celery sticks and tortilla chips for dipping.

CRAB & CITRUS SALSA

TZATZIKI

Place the yogurt, garlic, cucumber, oil, lemon juice, and mint in a serving bowl and stir together until well combined. Season to taste with salt and pepper, cover with plastic wrap, and let chill for at least 2 hours or until required.

When ready to serve, garnish with a pinch of paprika. Serve with carrot and celery stalks and pita bread triangles for dipping.

SERVES 4

scant 2½ cups plain
strained yogurt or other
thick plain yogurt

4 garlic cloves,
very finely chopped

2 medium cucumbers, peeled,
seeded, and very finely diced

1 tbsp lemon-flavored or extra
virgin olive oil

3 tbsp lemon juice

1 tbsp chopped fresh mint leaves

salt and pepper

pinch of paprika, to garnish

To serve

carrots, cut into short thin sticks

celery stalks, cut into short
thin sticks

pita breads, cut into triangles

CHORIZO & OLIVE FRITTATA

SERVES 4

4 tbsp butter

1 small onion, finely chopped

1 small green or red bell pepper, seeded and finely chopped

2 tomatoes, seeded and diced

2 small cooked potatoes, diced

4½ oz/125 g cured chorizo or salami, finely chopped

8 green or black olives, pitted and finely chopped

8 large eggs

2 tbsp milk

2 oz/55 g Cheddar cheese, grated

salt and pepper

To garnish
fresh mixed salad greens
pimiento strips

Melt the butter in a large skillet over medium heat. Add the onion, bell pepper, and tomatoes. Stir well to coat in butter, then cook for 3–4 minutes, or until soft. Mix in the potatoes, chorizo, and olives. Cook for 5 minutes to heat through.

In a small bowl, beat the eggs with the milk and salt and pepper to taste. Pour over the vegetables in the skillet and reduce the heat to low. Cook the eggs, occasionally lifting the edges and tilting the skillet to let the liquid run to the outside.

Preheat the broiler to high. When the eggs are mostly set, with only a small wet patch in the center, sprinkle over the cheese. Place the skillet under the broiler and cook for 2 minutes, or until the cheese has melted and is golden brown. Remove the skillet from the broiler and let the frittata cool before cutting into wedges. Garnish with salad greens and pimiento strips and serve.

OLIVE & TOMATO BRUSCHETTA

SERVES 4

½ cup extra virgin olive oil

1 small oval-shaped loaf white bread (ciabatta), cut into ½-inch/1-cm slices

4 tomatoes, seeded and diced

6 fresh basil leaves, torn

8 black olives, pitted and chopped

1 large garlic clove, peeled and halved

salt and pepper

Pour half the oil into a shallow dish and place the bread in it. Let stand for 1–2 minutes, then turn and let stand for an additional 2 minutes. The bread should be thoroughly saturated in oil.

Meanwhile, place the tomatoes in a bowl. Sprinkle the basil leaves over the tomatoes and season to taste with salt and pepper. Add the olives, then pour over the remaining oil and let marinate while you toast the bruschetta.

Preheat the broiler to medium. Place the bread on the broiler rack and cook for 2 minutes on each side, or until golden and crispy.

Remove the bread from the broiler and arrange on a serving dish.

Rub the cut edge of the garlic halves over the surface of the bruschetta, then top each slice with a spoonful of the tomato mixture. Serve as soon as possible.

JUMBO SHRIMP
WITH LEMON & LIME LEAF

SERVES 4 AS AN APPETIZER

12 large raw jumbo shrimp in their shells

Marinade
2 scallions, finely chopped

juice of ½ lemon

1 tsp chopped fresh lime leaf

1 tsp seeded and finely chopped fresh red chili or 1 tsp dried red pepper flakes

To serve
garlic mayonnaise

lemon wedges

Place the shrimp in a large bowl. Add the marinade ingredients and mix well. Cover the bowl with plastic wrap and let chill for 1 hour.

Preheat a stove-top grill pan over high heat and remove the shrimp from the refrigerator.

Cook the shrimp on the grill pan for 2–3 minutes on each side, turning once and ensuring that the shells are crispy and well browned.

Transfer the shrimp to a large serving dish. Serve at once with a bowl of garlic mayonnaise and lemon wedges.

SERVES 4

8 slices baguette or
ciabatta

4 oz/115 g Gorgonzola or
other strong blue cheese,
sliced or crumbled

4 fresh figs, thinly sliced

Preheat the broiler to medium. Place the bread on the
broiler rack and toast until golden on one side. Remove
the broiler rack from the heat.

Turn the bread over and sprinkle with the cheese, making
sure that it covers each slice right to the edge.

Arrange the figs on top of the cheese.

Return the rack to the broiler and cook for 3–4 minutes, or
until the cheese is soft and the fruit is hot. Transfer to an
attractive dish and serve at once.

FRESH FIGS
WITH GORGONZOLA

CLASSIC COCKTAIL

SERVES 1

1 lemon wedge

1 tsp superfine sugar

4–6 cracked ice cubes

2 measures brandy

½ measure clear curaçao

½ measure maraschino liqueur

½ measure lemon juice

1 lemon slice half, to decorate

Rub the rim of a chilled cocktail glass with the lemon wedge and then dip the rim in the sugar to frost.

Place the cracked ice in a cocktail shaker. Pour the brandy, curaçao, maraschino liqueur, and lemon juice over the ice and shake vigorously until a frost forms.

Strain into the frosted glass and decorate with the lemon slice half.

Variations

A number of cocktails are the quintessential classics of their type and named simply after the main ingredient.

Champagne Cocktail: place a sugar lump in the bottom of a chilled champagne flute and dash with angostura bitters to douse it. Fill the glass with chilled Champagne and decorate with a lemon peel twist.

Tequila Cocktail: place 4–6 cracked ice cubes in a cocktail shaker. Dash angostura bitters over the ice and pour in 3 measures golden tequila, 1 measure lime juice, and ½ measure grenadine. Shake vigorously until a frost forms, then strain into a chilled cocktail glass.

Variations

Duck's Fizz: use Canard-Duchêne Champagne.

Mimosa: pour the orange juice into the flute and then the Champagne. Stir gently. You can use sparkling white wine instead of Champagne.

Black Velvet: pour 1¼ cups chilled Champagne or sparkling white wine and 1¼ cups chilled stout into a chilled straight-sided glass together. Do not stir.

Soyer au Champagne: place 1 scoop vanilla ice cream in a wine glass and add ¼ teaspoon brandy, ¼ teaspoon Triple Sec, and ¼ teaspoon maraschino liqueur. Stir to mix, then top off with chilled Champagne. Stir gently and decorate with a maraschino cherry.

Champagne Cup: pour ½ measure brandy and ½ measure clear curaçao into a chilled wine glass. Add 1 ice cube and top off with Champagne. Decorate with a fresh mint sprig and an orange slice.

Spritzer: fill a wine glass with cracked ice cubes and pour in 3 measures white wine. Top off with club soda or sparkling mineral water and decorate with a lemon peel twist.

SERVES 1

2 measures chilled Champagne

2 measures chilled orange juice

Pour the Champagne into a chilled champagne flute, then pour in the orange juice.

BUCK'S FIZZ

4–6 cracked ice cubes

2 measures brandy

1 measure lemon juice

chilled Champagne, to top off

lemon peel twist, to decorate

sugar syrup

4 tbsp water

4 tbsp superfine sugar

To make sugar syrup, put the water and superfine sugar in a small pan and stir over low heat until the sugar has dissolved. Bring to a boil, then continue to boil, without stirring, for 1–2 minutes. Let cool, then set aside 1 tablespoon for the French 75 and chill the remainder in a covered container for future use. It should keep for up to 2 weeks.

Place the cracked ice cubes in a cocktail shaker. Pour the brandy, lemon juice, and reserved sugar syrup over the ice and shake vigorously until a frost forms.

Strain into a chilled highball glass and top off with chilled Champagne. Decorate with a lemon peel twist.

FRENCH 75

Variations

French 75 (second version): place 4–6 cracked ice cubes in a cocktail shaker. Pour 2 measures Plymouth gin and 1 measure lime juice over the ice and shake vigorously until a frost forms. Strain into a chilled wine glass and top off with chilled Champagne. Decorate with a maraschino cherry.

French 75 (third version): place 1 teaspoon superfine sugar in a chilled straight-sided glass. Add 1 measure lemon juice and stir until the sugar has dissolved. Fill the glass with cracked ice cubes. Pour 2 measures gin over the ice and top off with chilled Champagne. Decorate with orange slices and maraschino cherries.

London French 75: make the second version of a French 75, but substitute London gin for the Plymouth gin and lemon juice for the lime.

French Kiss: place 4–6 ice cubes in a cocktail shaker. Pour 2 measures bourbon, 1 measure apricot-flavored liqueur, 2 teaspoons grenadine, and 1 teaspoon lemon juice over the ice. Shake vigorously until a frost forms, then strain into a chilled cocktail glass.

French Rose: place 4–6 ice cubes in a mixing glass. Pour 2 measures gin, 1 measure kirsch, and 1 measure dry vermouth over the ice. Stir well and strain into a chilled cocktail glass.

2

SENSATIONAL SUMMER CELEBRATIONS

6 oz/175 g cantaloupe,
charentais, or galia melon

4 oz/115 g cucumber

large handful of fresh mint,
finely chopped

MINTED
MELON SALSA

Cut the flesh of the melon from its shell and remove and discard all the seeds.
Cut the flesh into tiny dice and place in a large bowl.

Cut the cucumber into quarters lengthwise and scrape away and discard any
seeds. Cut the flesh into tiny dice.

Add the cucumber to the melon with the mint and mix well. Let rest for
10 minutes before using.

Serve with griddled or pan-grilled fish or poultry.

SERVES 4 AS A SIDE DISH

1 lb/450 g ripe tomatoes, seeded and quartered

4 tbsp olive oil

2 tbsp red wine vinegar

2 tbsp finely snipped fresh chives

1 medium bunch fresh arugula or sorrel, finely chopped

1 medium bunch fresh cilantro, finely chopped

pinch of sugar

salt and pepper

TOMATO CILANTRO SALSA

Cut the tomato quarters into strips and place in a large bowl.

Add the oil and vinegar to the tomatoes and mix well.

Add the chives, arugula, and cilantro, then add the sugar and salt and pepper to taste and mix well. Let rest for 30 minutes before serving.

SERVES 4

3 tbsp olive oil

2 tbsp butter

2 garlic cloves, chopped

1 onion, chopped

2 large tomatoes,
seeded and diced

scant ¾ cup risotto rice

¾ cup frozen peas

1 red bell pepper,
seeded and chopped

2 tsp dried mixed herbs

1 tsp powdered saffron

scant 2 cups chicken stock

4 skinless, boneless
chicken breasts

5½ oz/150 g cured lean chorizo,
skinned

7 oz/200 g cooked lobster meat

7 oz/200 g raw shrimp,
peeled and deveined

1 tbsp chopped fresh
flat-leaf parsley

salt and pepper

To garnish

pinch of cayenne pepper

red bell pepper strips

Heat the oil and butter in a large skillet over medium heat. Add the garlic and onion and cook, stirring, for 3 minutes, or until slightly softened.

Add the tomatoes, rice, peas, bell pepper, mixed herbs, and saffron and cook, stirring, for 2 minutes. Pour in the stock and bring to a boil. Reduce the heat to low and cook, stirring, for 10 minutes.

Chop the chicken into bite-size chunks and add to the skillet. Cook, stirring occasionally, for 5 minutes. Chop the chorizo, add to the skillet, and cook for 3 minutes. Chop the lobster meat and add to the skillet with the shrimp and parsley. Season to taste with salt and pepper and cook, stirring, for an additional 3 minutes, or until the shrimp have turned pink.

Remove from the heat and transfer to a large serving platter or individual serving plates. Garnish with cayenne and bell pepper strips and serve at once.

PAELLA

ITALIAN
SALAD

BABY POTATO & SUN-DRIED TOMATO SALAD

8 oz/225 g dried conchiglie
(pasta shells)

scant ⅓ cup pine nuts

12 oz/350 g cherry tomatoes,
halved

1 red bell pepper, seeded and cut
into bite-size chunks

1 red onion, chopped

7 oz/200 g buffalo mozzarella,
cut into small pieces

12 black olives, pitted

2 tbsp fresh basil leaves

few fresh Parmesan cheese
shavings, to garnish

Dressing

5 tbsp extra virgin olive oil

2 tbsp balsamic vinegar

1 tbsp chopped fresh basil

salt and pepper

Bring a large pan of lightly salted water to a boil. Add the pasta and cook over medium heat for 10 minutes, or according to the package instructions. When cooked, the pasta should be tender but still firm to the bite. Drain, rinse under cold running water, and drain again. Let cool.

While the pasta is cooking, place the pine nuts in a dry skillet and cook over low heat for 1–2 minutes, or until golden brown. Remove from the heat, transfer to a dish, and let cool.

To make the dressing, place the oil, vinegar, and basil in a small bowl. Season to taste with salt and pepper and stir together well. Cover with plastic wrap and set aside.

To assemble the salad, divide the pasta between serving bowls. Add the pine nuts, tomatoes, bell pepper, onion, cheese, and olives. Sprinkle over the basil leaves, then drizzle over the dressing. Garnish with Parmesan cheese shavings and serve.

ITALIAN SALAD

BABY POTATO & SUN-DRIED TOMATO SALAD

SERVES 4

1 lb/450 g small new potatoes

1 tbsp sun-dried tomatoes

generous ⅓ cup cream cheese

1 tbsp olive oil

6 oz/175 g celery, sliced

2 scallions, sliced

1 medium carrot, grated

salt and pepper

Cook the potatoes in a large pan of lightly salted water for 15 minutes, or until tender.

Meanwhile, place the tomatoes in a heatproof bowl, cover with boiling water, and let stand for 10 minutes. In a separate bowl, mix the cream cheese and salt and pepper to taste together for the dressing.

Drain the cooked potatoes and place in a salad bowl. Add the oil and toss together. Drain the tomatoes and thinly slice. Add to the potatoes with the celery, scallions, and carrot.

Drizzle the dressing over the salad and toss together. Cover with plastic wrap and let chill for 1 hour before serving.

MIXED CABBAGE
COLESLAW
WITH FRUIT

Wash and shred the white and red cabbage. Grate the carrots and finely chop the onion. Place all the prepared vegetables in a large salad bowl, then wash the golden raisins and raisins and add them to the bowl.

In a separate bowl, mix the mayonnaise and lemon juice together, season to taste with salt and pepper, and pour over the salad. Mix all the ingredients together until well combined. Serve at once or cover with plastic wrap and let chill until required.

SERVES 4

3½ oz/100 g white cabbage

3½ oz/100 g red cabbage

2 large carrots

1 onion

generous ⅛ cup golden raisins

generous ⅛ cup raisins

generous ⅓ cup mayonnaise

2 tbsp lemon juice

salt and pepper

SERVES 4

1 lb/450 g canned Great Northern
beans, drained

12 oz/350 g canned chickpeas,
drained

1 onion, finely chopped

2 garlic cloves, chopped

1 small fresh red chili,
seeded and chopped

1 tsp baking powder

scant ½ cup chopped fresh parsley

pinch of cayenne pepper

2 tbsp water

salt and pepper

vegetable oil, for deep-frying

fresh parsley sprigs, to garnish

Sesame seed sauce

scant 1 cup sesame seed paste

1 garlic clove, chopped

1–2 tbsp water

2–3 tsp lemon juice

To serve

lemon wedges

pita breads

thick plain yogurt or Tzatziki
(see page 35)

FALAFEL

To make the sesame seed sauce, place the sesame seed paste in a bowl, then add the garlic. Gradually stir in the water until a fairly smooth consistency is reached, then stir in lemon juice to taste. Add more water or lemon juice if necessary. Cover with plastic wrap and let chill until required.

To make the falafel, rinse and drain the beans and chickpeas. Place in a food processor with the onion, garlic, chili, baking powder, parsley, and cayenne. Process to a coarse paste, then add the water and season with plenty of salt and pepper. Process again briefly.

Heat about 2½ inches/6 cm of oil in a deep-fryer or a large, heavy-bottom pan to 350–375°F/180–190°C, or until a cube of bread browns in 30 seconds. Deep-fry rounded tablespoonfuls of the mixture, in batches, in the hot oil for 2–2½ minutes, or until golden and crispy on the outside. Drain well on paper towels and garnish with parsley sprigs. Serve hot or cold with the sesame seed sauce, lemon wedges, pita breads, and yogurt.

BITE-SIZE BARBECUED SPARERIBS

SERVES 4

2 lb 4 oz/1 kg spareribs, chopped into 2-inch/5-cm pieces

3 tbsp torn fresh cilantro, to garnish

Sauce

¼ cup plum, hoisin, sweet-&-sour, or duck sauce

1 tsp brown sugar

1 tbsp tomato ketchup

pinch of garlic powder

2 tbsp dark soy sauce

Preheat the oven to 375°F/190°C.

To make the sauce, combine all the ingredients in a large bowl.

Add the spareribs to the sauce and stir to coat them thoroughly. Transfer to a metal roasting pan and arrange in a single layer.

Transfer the roasting pan to the oven and cook the ribs for 20 minutes, or until they are cooked right through and sticky. Arrange on a large platter and serve at once, garnished with cilantro.

CHERRY TOMATO, HAM & PINEAPPLE SKEWERS

SERVES 4

1 tbsp vegetable oil

1 tbsp white wine vinegar

1 tsp mustard powder

1 tbsp honey

1 lb/450 g ham, cubed

1 lb/450 g canned pineapple chunks, drained

12 cherry tomatoes

freshly cooked rice, fresh green lettuce leaves, or fresh crusty bread, to serve

Place the oil, vinegar, mustard powder, and honey in a bowl and mix until well combined.

Thread the ham onto skewers (presoaked in water for 30 minutes if wooden or bamboo), alternating with pineapple chunks and whole tomatoes. When the skewers are full (leave a small space at either end), brush them with the honey mixture until they are well coated.

Barbecue the skewers over hot coals, turning them frequently, for 10 minutes, or until the ham is cooked right through. Serve with rice, green lettuce leaves, or crusty bread.

SERVES 6

10½ oz/300 g fresh tuna steaks

9 lb/250 g white mushrooms

chopped fresh tarragon, to garnish

Marinade

2 tbsp white wine

3 tbsp balsamic vinegar

1 tbsp extra virgin olive oil

1 garlic clove, finely chopped

salt and pepper

To serve

freshly cooked rice

fresh mixed salad

TUNA & TARRAGON
SKEWERS

To make the marinade, place the wine, vinegar, oil, and garlic in a large bowl and
mix until well combined. Season to taste with salt and pepper.

Rinse the tuna steaks under cold running water and pat dry with paper towels.
Cut them into small cubes. Wipe the mushrooms clean with paper towels. Thread
the tuna cubes onto skewers (presoaked in water for 30 minutes if wooden or
bamboo), alternating with the whole mushrooms. When the skewers are full
(leave a small space at either end), transfer to the bowl, and turn them in the
wine mixture until they are well coated. Cover with plastic wrap and place in the
refrigerator to marinate for at least 30 minutes.

Barbecue the skewers over hot coals for 10 minutes, or until the tuna is cooked
right through (but do not overcook), turning them frequently and basting with
the remaining marinade. Arrange the skewers on a bed of rice, garnish with
chopped tarragon, and serve with a mixed salad.

1 small onion, finely chopped

1 tbsp chopped fresh cilantro

¼ tsp ground coriander

large pinch of paprika

¼ tsp allspice

¼ tsp brown sugar

1 lb/450 g fresh ground beef

salt and pepper

vegetable oil, for brushing

fresh cilantro leaves, to garnish

To serve

freshly cooked bulgur wheat
or rice

fresh mixed salad

GREEK-STYLE BEEF KABOBS

Place the onion, fresh cilantro, spices, sugar, and beef in a large bowl and mix until well combined. Season to taste with salt and pepper.

On a clean counter, use your hands to shape the mixture into sausages around skewers (presoaked in water for 30 minutes if wooden or bamboo). Brush lightly with oil.

Barbecue the kabobs over hot coals, turning them frequently, for 15–20 minutes, or until cooked right through. Arrange the kabobs on a platter of bulgur wheat and garnish with cilantro. Serve with a mixed salad.

MINIATURE CHICKEN KABOBS

SERVES 4

1 chicken breast, skinned, boned, and cut into ½-inch/1-cm pieces

½ small onion, cut into ½-inch/1-cm pieces

½ red bell pepper, cut into ½-inch/1-cm pieces

½ green bell pepper, cut into ½-inch/1-cm pieces

Sweet & sour marinade

½ cup orange, grapefruit, or pineapple juice

1 tbsp sweet sherry

¼ cup dark soy sauce

¼ cup chicken stock

2 tbsp apple cider vinegar

1 tsp tomato paste

2 tbsp brown sugar

pinch of ground ginger

To make the marinade, combine all the liquid ingredients in a large bowl. Add the tomato paste, sugar, and ginger. Mix well, then add the chicken and vegetables and stir to coat thoroughly. Cover the bowl with plastic wrap and place in the refrigerator to marinate for 30 minutes.

Drain off the marinade and set aside. Thread alternating pieces of chicken and vegetables onto soaked wooden toothpicks, taking care not to pack them together tightly.

Preheat a stove-top grill pan or heavy-bottom skillet over high heat. Cook the kabobs on the pan, turning frequently, for 10 minutes, or until lightly browned and cooked right through. Baste occasionally with the reserved marinade.

Pile the kabobs high on a serving platter and serve at once.

BEAN & VEGETABLE BURGERS
WITH TOMATO SALSA

SERVES 4

7 oz/200 g canned chickpeas, drained

7 oz/200 g canned cannellini beans, drained

1 large zucchini, finely grated

1 large carrot, finely grated

1 garlic clove, finely chopped

1½ cups fresh bread crumbs

salt and pepper

lime wedges, to garnish

hamburger buns, to serve

Salsa

4 large tomatoes, chopped

1 tbsp lime juice

2 shallots, chopped

1 garlic clove, chopped

1 tbsp chopped fresh basil, plus extra to garnish

Rinse and drain the chickpeas and beans, then place in a food processor and blend together briefly. Transfer to a large bowl, then add the zucchini, carrot, garlic, and bread crumbs. Season to taste with salt and pepper, then mix together until thoroughly combined. Using your hands, form the mixture into burger shapes, transfer to a shallow dish, and cover with plastic wrap. Let chill for 30 minutes.

To make the salsa, place all the ingredients in a bowl and stir together. Cover with plastic wrap and set aside.

Barbecue the burgers over hot coals for 5–10 minutes on each side, or until cooked right through. Transfer to serving plates, garnish with chopped basil and lime wedges, and serve with hamburger buns and the salsa.

Place the garlic, onion, chili, pork, tomatoes, breadcrumbs, and thyme in a large bowl. Season well with salt and pepper and mix with the hands to combine.

Using your hands, form the mixture into sausage shapes. Roll until neatly shaped. Place them in a cool place and leave to firm up for at least 5 minutes.

Brush a piece of foil with oil, then place the sausages on the foil and brush with a little more oil. Transfer the sausages and foil to the barbecue to cook over hot coals, turning the sausages frequently for 15 minutes, or until cooked right through. Serve with rolls, cooked onion slices, and tomato ketchup.

BARBECUED
PORK SAUSAGES
WITH THYME

HAMBURGERS
WITH CHILI & BASIL

SERVES 4

1 lb 7 oz/650 g fresh ground beef

1 red bell pepper, seeded and
finely chopped

1 garlic clove, finely chopped

2 small fresh red chilies, seeded
and finely chopped

1 tbsp chopped fresh basil

½ tsp ground cumin

salt and pepper

fresh basil sprigs, to garnish

hamburger buns, to serve

Place the beef, bell pepper, garlic, chilies, basil, and cumin in a
bowl and mix until well combined. Season to taste with salt
and pepper.

Using your hands, form the mixture into burger shapes. Barbecue
the burgers over hot coals for 5–8 minutes on each side, or until
cooked right through. Garnish with basil sprigs and serve with
hamburger buns.

GREEK SALAD

SERVES 4

4 tomatoes, cut into wedges

1 onion, sliced

½ cucumber, sliced

1⅓ cups kalamata olives, pitted

8 oz/225 g feta cheese (drained weight), cubed

2 tbsp chopped fresh cilantro leaves

fresh flat-leaf parsley sprigs, to garnish

pita breads, to serve

Dressing

5 tbsp extra virgin olive oil

2 tbsp white wine vinegar

1 tbsp lemon juice

½ tsp sugar

1 tbsp chopped fresh cilantro

salt and pepper

To make the dressing, place the oil, vinegar, lemon juice, sugar, and cilantro in a large bowl. Season to taste with salt and pepper and mix together well.

Add the tomatoes, onion, cucumber, olives, cheese, and cilantro. Toss all the ingredients together, then divide between individual serving bowls. Garnish with parsley sprigs and serve with pita breads.

Cutting close to the seed, cut a large slice from one side of the mango, then cut another slice from the opposite side. Without breaking the skin, cut the flesh in the segments into squares, then push the skin inside out to expose the cubes and cut away from the skin. Use a sharp knife to peel the remaining center section and cut the flesh away from the seed into cubes. Set aside any juice and place in a serving bowl with the mango flesh.

Cut the papaya in half and remove and discard the seeds. Remove the skin and cut the flesh into cubes. Peel the pineapple, remove the center core and as many "eyes" as possible, and cut the flesh into chunks. Add both fruits to the mango.

Pour over the fruit juice, cover with plastic wrap, and let the mixture chill for about 1 hour. Just before serving, peel and slice the bananas, then add the slices to the fruit salad.

TROPICAL FRUIT SALAD

SERVES 4

1 ripe mango

1 papaya

1 small pineapple

1½ cups pineapple
or orange juice

2 small bananas

SERVES 4

6 tbsp butter

1–2 tbsp brown sugar

pinch of allspice

1/2 melon, such as cantaloupe or galia, seeded

2 red-skinned eating apples

1 tbsp lemon juice

plain yogurt, sour cream, mascarpone cheese, or ice cream, to serve

APPLE & MELON KABOBS

In a small pan, melt the butter gently over low heat. Stir in the sugar and allspice, then remove from the heat and pour into a large bowl.

Cut the melon flesh into small chunks. Wash and core the apples, and cut into small chunks. Brush the fruit with lemon juice to prevent discoloration.

Thread the melon chunks onto skewers (presoaked in water for 30 minutes if wooden or bamboo), alternating with pieces of apple. When the skewers are full (leave a small space at either end), transfer to the bowl, and turn them in the butter mixture until they are well coated.

Barbecue the kabobs over hot coals, turning them frequently, for about 10 minutes, or until they are cooked to your taste. Serve with plain yogurt.

BARBECUED APPLES

SERVES 4

4 firm eating apples, such as Granny Smith

3 tbsp lemon juice

3 tbsp butter

4 tsp brown sugar

8 tbsp sweet mincemeat

plain yogurt, sour cream, or mascarpone cheese, to serve

Wash the apples, then cut them in half from top to bottom. Remove and discard the cores and pips, then brush the cut sides of the apples with lemon juice to prevent discoloration.

Place the butter in a small pan and gently melt it over low heat. Remove from the heat, then brush the cut sides of the apples with half the butter. Set aside the remainder of the melted butter.

Sprinkle the apples with the sugar, then transfer them to the barbecue, cut-sides down, and cook over hot coals for about 5 minutes. Brush the apples with the remaining butter, then turn them over. Add a tablespoon of mincemeat to the center of each apple, then cook for an additional 5 minutes, or until they are cooked to your taste.

Remove from the heat and transfer to serving plates. Serve with plain yogurt.

CHOCOLATE
RUM BANANAS

CHERRY SODA

CHOCOLATE RUM BANANAS

Take four 10-inch/25-cm squares of foil and brush them with the butter.

Cut the chocolate into very small pieces. Make a careful slit lengthwise in the skin of each banana and open just wide enough to insert the chocolate. Place the chocolate pieces inside the bananas, along their lengths, then close them up.

Wrap each stuffed banana in a square of foil, then barbecue them over hot coals for 5–10 minutes, or until the chocolate has melted inside the bananas. Remove from the barbecue, place the bananas on individual serving plates, and pour some rum into each banana. Serve at once with sour cream, decorated with nutmeg.

SERVES 4

1 tbsp butter, melted

8 oz/225 g semisweet or milk chocolate

4 large bananas

2 tbsp rum

freshly grated nutmeg, to decorate

sour cream, mascarpone cheese, or ice cream, to serve

CHERRY SODA

Divide the crushed ice between 2 glasses and pour over the cherry syrup.

Top off each glass with sparkling mineral water. Decorate with the maraschino cherries on toothpicks and serve.

SERVES 2

8 ice cubes, crushed

2 tbsp cherry syrup

scant 2½ cups sparkling mineral water

To decorate

maraschino cherries on toothpicks

SERVES 2

²⁄₃ cup water

6 tbsp sugar

1 tsp grated lemon rind

½ cup lemon juice

6 ice cubes

To decorate

1 lemon wedge

granulated sugar

lemon slices

To serve

sparkling mineral water

Place the water, sugar, and lemon rind in a small pan and bring to a boil, stirring constantly. Continue to boil, stirring, for 5 minutes.

Remove from the heat and let cool to room temperature. Stir in the lemon juice, then transfer to a pitcher, cover with plastic wrap, and let chill for at least 2 hours.

When the lemonade has almost finished chilling, take 2 glasses and rub the rims with a lemon wedge, then dip them in the sugar to frost. Place the ice cubes in the glasses.

Remove the lemon syrup from the refrigerator, pour it over the ice, and top off with sparkling mineral water. The ratio should be 1 part lemon syrup to 3 parts sparkling water. Stir well to mix, decorate with lemon slices, and serve.

HOMEMADE LEMONADE

PINEAPPLE FLOAT

SERVES 2

¾ **cup pineapple juice**

generous ⅓ cup coconut milk

⅞ **cup vanilla ice cream**

**5 oz/140 g frozen
pineapple chunks**

¾ **cup sparkling
mineral water**

To serve

**2 scooped-out pineapple shells
(optional)**

Pour the pineapple juice and coconut milk into a food processor. Add the ice cream and process until smooth.

Add the pineapple chunks and process well. Pour the mixture into scooped-out pineapple shells, if using, or tall glasses, until two-thirds full. Top off with sparkling mineral water, add straws, and serve.

3

WONDERFUL WINTER WARMERS

Firmly holding each bacon slice down in turn with a knife or fork on a cutting board, use a sharp knife to smooth and stretch the length.

Place a date at one end of each slice and roll up. Secure with a toothpick to keep it closed.

Preheat a ridged stove-top grill pan or broiler until very hot. Place the bacon rolls on the grill pan or on the broiler rack and cook, turning once, for 5–10 minutes, or until the bacon is crisp and well-browned. Whatever is wrapped in the bacon must be thoroughly cooked or heated through. Alternatively, you could cook the bacon rolls on a baking sheet for 25–30 minutes in an oven preheated to 400°F /200°C.

Transfer to a large platter and serve at once.

CRISPY BACON NIBBLES

SERVES 4

12 lean bacon slices

12 pitted dates or prunes,
or raw scallops
or water chestnuts

OVEN-FRIED CHICKEN WINGS

SERVES 4

12 chicken wings

¼ cup milk

4 heaping tbsp all-purpose flour

1 tsp paprika

1 egg

4 cups fresh bread crumbs

2 oz/55 g butter

salt and pepper

Preheat the oven to 425°F/220°C.

Separate the wings into 3 pieces each. Remove and discard the bony tips. Beat the egg with the milk in a shallow dish. Combine the flour, paprika, and salt and pepper to taste in a separate shallow dish. Place the bread crumbs in another shallow dish.

Dip the chicken pieces into the egg, coat well, then drain and dredge in flour. Remove, shaking off any excess, and roll in the bread crumbs, pressing them in gently, then shaking off any excess.

Melt the butter in the oven in a shallow roasting pan large enough to hold all the chicken pieces in a single layer. Arrange the chicken, skin-side down, in the butter and bake for 10 minutes. Turn and bake for an additional 10 minutes.

Remove the chicken from the pan and arrange on a large platter. Serve hot or at room temperature.

SERVES 4

1 lb 2 oz/500 g salmon fillet, skinned

2 tbsp sea salt

1 tbsp superfine sugar

2 tbsp chopped fresh dill

1 tbsp chopped fresh tarragon

1 tsp Dijon mustard

juice of 1 lemon

pepper

fresh dill sprigs, to garnish

Topping

1³/₄ cups cream cheese

1 tbsp snipped fresh chives

pinch of paprika

SALMON TARTARE

Place the salmon in a shallow glass dish. Combine the salt, sugar, and dill, then rub into the salmon until well coated. Season with plenty of pepper. Cover with plastic wrap and let chill for at least 48 hours, turning the salmon once.

When ready to serve, place the tarragon in a bowl with the mustard and lemon juice. Season well. Remove the salmon from the refrigerator, chop into small pieces, then add to the bowl. Stir until the salmon is well coated.

To make the topping, place all the ingredients in a separate bowl and mix well. Place a 4-inch/10-cm steel cooking ring or round cookie cutter on each of 4 small serving plates. Divide the salmon between the 4 rings so that each ring is half-full. Level the surface of each one, then top with the cream cheese mixture. Smooth the surfaces, then carefully remove the steel rings. Garnish with dill sprigs and serve.

GARLIC MUSHROOMS
WITH WHITE WINE & CHESTNUTS

SWISS-STYLE FONDUE
WITH BRANDY

SERVES 4

4 tbsp butter

4 garlic cloves, chopped

**7 oz/200 g button mushrooms,
sliced**

**7 oz/200 g cremini mushrooms,
sliced**

4 tbsp dry white wine

generous ⅓ cup heavy cream

**10½ oz/300 g canned whole
chestnuts, drained**

**3½ oz/100 g chanterelle
mushrooms, sliced**

salt and pepper

chopped fresh parsley, to garnish

Melt the butter in a large pan over medium heat. Add the garlic and cook, stirring, for 3 minutes, or until softened. Add the button and cremini mushrooms and cook for an additional 3 minutes.

Stir in the wine and cream and season to taste with salt and pepper. Cook for 2 minutes, stirring, then add the chestnuts and the chanterelle mushrooms. Cook for an additional 2 minutes, stirring, then remove from the heat and transfer to a serving dish. Garnish with chopped parsley and serve.

GARLIC
MUSHROOMS
WITH WHITE WINE & CHESTNUTS

SWISS-STYLE FONDUE
WITH BRANDY

SERVES 4

1 garlic clove, peeled and halved

scant 2 cups dry white wine

5 tbsp brandy

1¾ cups grated Gruyère cheese

1¾ cups grated Emmental cheese

1¾ cups grated Comté cheese,

1 scant cup grated Parmesan cheese

2 tbsp cornstarch

pinch of freshly grated nutmeg

salt and pepper

Dippers

fresh crusty bread, cut into bite-size pieces

small pieces of blanched asparagus

Rub the inside of an ovenproof fondue pot with the garlic. Discard the garlic. Pour in the wine and 3 tablespoons of the brandy, then transfer to the stove and bring to a gentle simmer over low heat.

Mix the cheeses together in a bowl. Add a small handful to the fondue and stir constantly until melted. Continue to add the cheese gradually, stirring constantly after each addition. Repeat until all the cheese has been added and stir until thoroughly melted and bubbling gently.

In a separate bowl, mix the cornstarch with the remaining brandy. Stir the cornstarch mixture into the fondue and continue to stir for 3–4 minutes, or until thickened and bubbling. Stir in the nutmeg and season to taste with salt and pepper.

Using protective gloves, transfer the fondue pot to a lit tabletop burner. To serve, "invite" your guests to spear pieces of bread and asparagus onto fondue forks and dip them into the fondue.

Preheat the oven to 375°F/190°C.

Prick the potatoes with a fork and place on a baking sheet. Brush with oil and sprinkle with salt. Bake in the oven for 1 hour, or until the skins are crispy and the flesh is soft when pierced with a fork.

Melt 1 tablespoon of the butter in a small skillet. Add the onion and cook gently until soft and golden. Set aside.

Remove the potatoes from the oven and cut in half lengthwise. Scoop out the flesh into a large bowl and set aside the shells. Increase the oven temperature to 400°F/200°C.

Coarsely mash the potato and mix in the onion and remaining butter. Add salt and pepper to taste and any of the optional ingredients. Spoon the mixture back into the empty shells. Top with cheese.

Return the potatoes to the oven for 10 minutes, or until the cheese melts and starts to brown. Garnish with chives and serve at once.

STUFFED BAKED POTATOES

SERVES 4

2 lb/900 g baking potatoes, scrubbed

2 tbsp vegetable oil

1 tsp coarse sea salt

4 oz/115 g butter

1 small onion, chopped

1 cup grated Cheddar cheese or crumbled blue cheese

salt and pepper

fresh chives, to garnish

Optional

4 tbsp cooked ham or bacon, diced

4 tbsp corn kernels

4 tbsp cooked mushrooms, zucchini, or bell peppers

WINTER MINESTRONE
WITH SAUSAGES

SERVES 4

3 tbsp olive oil

9 oz/250 g coarse-textured pork sausages, skinned and cut into chunks

1 onion, thinly sliced

2 garlic cloves, very finely chopped

1 cup canned chopped tomatoes

2 tbsp chopped fresh mixed herbs, such as flat-leaf parsley, sage, and marjoram

1 celery stalk, thinly sliced

1 carrot, diced

1 small red bell pepper, seeded and diced

3½ cups chicken stock

½ cup short macaroni

¼ cup canned Great Northern beans, drained

1 cup frozen peas

2 tbsp freshly grated Parmesan, plus extra to serve

salt and pepper

4 thick slices ciabatta or French bread, to serve

Heat the oil in a large pan over medium–low heat. Add the sausage and onion and cook, stirring occasionally, until the onion is just colored.

Add the garlic, tomatoes, and herbs and cook for 5 minutes, stirring. Add the celery, carrot, and bell pepper, cover, and cook for 5 minutes.

Pour in the stock. Bring to a boil, then cover and simmer gently for 30 minutes.

Season to taste with salt and pepper. Add the macaroni and beans and let simmer for 15 minutes, or until the macaroni is just tender.

Stir in the peas and cook for an additional 5 minutes. Stir in the 2 tablespoons of Parmesan cheese.

To serve, place the bread in individual serving bowls. Ladle the hot soup over the bread and let stand for a few minutes. Serve with plenty of extra Parmesan cheese.

SERVES 4

3 tbsp olive oil

1 lb 10 oz/750 g lean stewing
steak, cubed

2 garlic cloves, chopped

1 large onion, chopped

9 oz/250 g white mushrooms,
sliced

4 large tomatoes,
peeled and chopped

2 carrots, sliced

6 black olives,
pitted and quartered

6 green olives,
pitted and quartered

1¼ cups red wine

scant 1 cup vegetable stock

salt and pepper

2 fresh flat-leaf parsley sprigs,
to garnish

fresh crusty bread, to serve

PROVENÇAL STEW

Preheat the oven to 325°F/
160°C.

Heat 2 tablespoons of the oil in an
ovenproof casserole over high
heat. Add the meat and cook,
stirring, for 5 minutes, or until
sealed. Remove from the heat.
Using a slotted spoon, lift out the
meat and set aside.

Heat the remaining oil in the
casserole over medium heat.
Add the garlic and onion and cook,
stirring, for 4 minutes, or until
slightly softened. Add the
mushrooms and tomatoes and
cook for an additional 5 minutes,
stirring frequently.

Return the meat to the casserole,
then add the carrots and olives
and season to taste with salt and
pepper. Pour in the wine and stock
and bring to a boil. Reduce the
heat, cover, and let simmer for
15 minutes. Transfer to the oven
and cook for 1½ hours. Garnish
with a parsley sprig and serve with
crusty bread.

FESTIVE BEEF
WELLINGTON

SERVES 4

1 lb 10 oz/750 g tenderloin

2 tbsp butter

2 tbsp vegetable oil

1 garlic clove, chopped

1 onion, chopped

6 oz/175 g cremini mushrooms, chopped

1 tbsp chopped fresh sage, plus extra to garnish

12 oz/350 g frozen puff pastry, thawed

1 egg, beaten

salt and pepper

To serve

roast potatoes

Garlic Mushrooms with White Wine & Chestnuts (see page 90)

freshly cooked Brussels sprouts

Preheat the oven to 425°F/220°C. Put the beef in a roasting pan, spread with the butter, and season. Roast for 30 minutes, then remove from the oven. Meanwhile, heat the oil in a pan over medium heat. Add the garlic and onion and cook, stirring, for 3 minutes. Stir in the mushrooms and sage and cook for 5 minutes. Remove from the heat.

Roll out the pastry into a rectangle large enough to enclose the beef, then place the beef in the center and spread the mushroom mixture over it. Bring the long sides of the pastry together over the beef and seal with beaten egg. Tuck the short ends over (trim away any excess pastry) and seal. Place on a baking sheet, seam-side down. Make 2 slits in the top. Decorate with pastry shapes and brush with beaten egg. Bake for 40 minutes. If the pastry browns too quickly, cover with foil. Remove from the oven, garnish with sage, and serve with roast potatoes, Garlic Mushrooms with White Wine & Chestnuts, and sprouts.

Preheat the oven to 375°F/190°C.

In a small bowl, mix 1 tablespoon of the butter with the garlic, walnuts, and parsley. Season well with salt and pepper. Loosen the skin from the breast of the chicken without breaking it. Spread the butter mixture evenly between the skin and breast meat. Place the lime quarters inside the body cavity.

Pour the oil into a roasting pan. Transfer the chicken to the pan and dot the skin with the remaining butter. Roast for 1¾ hours, basting occasionally, until the chicken is tender and the juices run clear when a skewer is inserted into the thickest part of the meat. Lift out and place on a serving platter to rest for 10 minutes.

Blend the cornstarch with the water, then stir into the juices in the pan. Transfer to the stove. Stir over low heat until thickened. Add more water if necessary. Garnish the chicken with lime wedges and rosemary sprigs. Serve with roast potatoes, a selection of cooked vegetables, and the thickened juices.

SERVES 4

2 tbsp butter, softened

1 garlic clove, finely chopped

3 tbsp finely chopped toasted walnuts

1 tbsp chopped fresh parsley

1 chicken, weighing 4 lb/1.8 kg

1 lime, quartered

2 tbsp vegetable oil

1 tbsp cornstarch

2 tbsp water

salt and pepper

To garnish
lime wedges
fresh rosemary sprigs

To serve
roast potatoes
selection of freshly cooked vegetables

TRADITIONAL ROAST CHICKEN

Preheat the oven to 400°F/200°C.

Pour the oil into a roasting pan. Using a sharp knife, trim off and discard any excess fat from the lamb, then make small incisions all over. Transfer the joint to the roasting pan. Place the garlic in a bowl and add the oregano, lemon juice, maple syrup, and salt and pepper to taste. Mix together well. Pour the mixture evenly over the lamb, pushing it into the incisions, then pour over the cider.

Transfer the pan to the oven and roast for 30 minutes, turning once and basting occasionally. Reduce the oven temperature to 300°F/150°C and cook for an additional 2¾ hours, or until tender and cooked through. Lift out and place on a serving platter to rest for 10 minutes. Blend the cornstarch with the water, then stir into the juices in the pan. Transfer to the stove. Stir over low heat until thickened. Garnish the lamb with oregano sprigs. Serve with roast potatoes, a selection of cooked vegetables, and the thickened juices.

SERVES 4

2 tbsp lemon-flavored oil or extra virgin olive oil

5 lb/2.25 kg leg of lamb

1 garlic clove, chopped

1 tbsp chopped fresh oregano

juice of 1 lemon

3 tbsp maple syrup

3 cups hard cider

1 tbsp cornstarch

2 tbsp water

salt and pepper

fresh oregano sprigs, to garnish

MAPLE ROAST LAMB
WITH CIDER

To serve
roast potatoes
selection of freshly cooked vegetables

SERVES 4

1 lb/450 g frozen crabmeat, thawed

2 tbsp freshly grated lime rind

1 fresh red chili, seeded and finely chopped

1 tbsp finely chopped scallion

1 tbsp grated fresh gingerroot

1 tbsp grated fresh coconut

2 egg yolks

4 tsp cornstarch

4 tbsp thick plain yogurt

2 tbsp sherry

salt and pepper

4 cups peanut oil

Dippers

7 oz/200 g firm tofu (drained weight), cut into bite-size pieces

selection of vegetables, cut into bite-size pieces

To serve

Red Chili Dipping Sauce (see page 126)

freshly cooked rice

Place the crabmeat, lime rind, chili, scallion, ginger, coconut, and egg yolks in a bowl and mix together well. Mix the cornstarch with the yogurt and sherry in a small pan, place over low heat, and stir until thickened. Remove from the heat, mix into the bowl with the crabmeat mixture, and season to taste with salt and pepper. Pull off pieces of the mixture and shape into 1-inch/2.5-cm balls. Cover with plastic wrap and let chill for at least 1 hour. Arrange the other dippers on serving plates.

Pour the oil into a metal fondue pot (It should be no more than one-third full), then heat on the stove to 350–375°F/180–190°C, or until a cube of bread browns in 30 seconds. Using protective gloves, carefully transfer the fondue pot to a lit tabletop burner. To serve, "invite" your guests to spear the dippers onto fondue forks (place the crab balls on spoons if not firm enough to spear), then cook in the hot oil for about 2–3 minutes, or until cooked to their taste. Drain off the excess oil, then serve with the dipping sauce and rice.

SPICED CRAB BALLS

SNOWY CHOCOLATE CRISPIES

MAKES 24 CRISPIES

8 oz/225 g butter

⁷/₈ cup corn syrup

8 oz/225 g semisweet chocolate, chopped into small pieces

7 oz/200 g puffed rice cereal

8 oz/225 g white chocolate, chopped into small pieces

In a small pan, gently warm the butter and corn syrup over low heat, until the butter has melted. Add the semisweet chocolate and stir until it has melted.

Remove from the heat and add the puffed rice. Stir thoroughly to ensure that the rice is evenly coated. Spoon the mixture into 24 little muffin cases and set aside to set for 5 minutes.

Meanwhile, place the white chocolate in a heatproof bowl set over a pan of barely simmering water and heat until melted. Pour a teaspoonful of melted chocolate on top of each cake and let set for at least 5 minutes before serving.

In a large bowl, sift the flour, baking soda, ginger, allspice, and salt together. In a separate bowl, beat the butter, corn syrup, raw brown sugar, egg, and brandy together until thoroughly combined. Gradually stir in the orange rind, then the flour mixture.

Halve the dough, then wrap in plastic wrap and let chill for at least 4 hours (it will keep for up to 6 days). When ready to use, preheat the oven to 350°F/180°C. Grease a baking sheet.

Flour a board or counter. Roll each half of dough into a ball, then roll it to a thickness of ⅛ inch/3 mm. Using cookie cutters or a knife, cut shapes such as stars and trees. Place the cookies on the baking sheet, transfer to the oven, and bake for 10 minutes, or until golden brown. Remove the cookies from the oven, transfer to a wire rack, and set aside. When the cookies have cooled completely, dredge over confectioners' sugar or drizzle over a little frosting and serve.

MAKES 30 COOKIES

generous 2⅜ cups self-rising flour, plus extra for dusting

1 tsp baking soda

1 tbsp ground ginger

3 tsp allspice

pinch of salt

4½ oz/125 g butter or margarine, plus extra for greasing

5 tbsp corn syrup

1 cup raw brown sugar

1 egg

1 tsp brandy

1 tsp very finely grated orange rind

confectioners' sugar or frosting, to decorate

YULETIDE COOKIES

PROFITEROLES

FESTIVE SHERRY TRIFLE

PROFITEROLES

SERVES 4

Choux pastry

5 tbsp butter, plus extra
for greasing

scant 1 cup water

scant ¾ cup all-purpose flour

3 eggs, beaten

Cream filling

1¼ cups heavy cream

3 tbsp superfine sugar

1 tsp vanilla extract

Chocolate & brandy sauce

4½ oz/125 g semisweet chocolate,
broken into small pieces

2½ tbsp butter

6 tbsp water

2 tbsp brandy

Preheat the oven to 400°F/200°C. Grease a large baking sheet.

To make the pastry, place the water and butter in a pan and bring to a boil. Meanwhile, sift the flour into a bowl. Remove the pan from the heat and beat in the flour until smooth. Let cool for 5 minutes. Beat in enough of the eggs to give the mixture a soft, dropping consistency. Transfer to a pastry bag fitted with a ½-inch/1-cm plain tip. Pipe small balls onto the baking sheet, transfer to the oven, and bake for 25 minutes. Remove from the oven. Pierce each ball with a skewer to let the steam escape.

To make the filling, whip the cream, sugar, and vanilla extract together in a bowl. When cool, cut the pastry balls almost in half, then fill with the cream.

To make the sauce, gently melt the chocolate and butter with the water in a small pan, stirring, until smooth. Stir in the brandy. Pile the profiteroles into individual serving dishes or into a pyramid on a raised cake stand. Pour over the sauce and serve.

SERVES 4

Fruit layer

3½ oz/100 g ladyfingers

⅔ cup raspberry preserves

scant 1¼ cups sherry

scant ¾ cup frozen raspberries, thawed

14 oz/400 g canned mixed fruit, drained

1 large banana, sliced

Custard layer

6 egg yolks

¼ cup superfine sugar

scant 2½ cups milk

1 tsp vanilla extract

Topping

1¼ cups heavy cream

1–2 tbsp superfine sugar

toasted mixed nuts, chopped, to decorate

Spread the ladyfingers with preserves, cut them into bite-size cubes, and arrange in the bottom of a large glass serving bowl. Pour over the sherry and let stand for 30 minutes.

Combine the raspberries, canned fruit, and banana and arrange over the ladyfingers. Cover with plastic wrap and let chill for 30 minutes.

To make the custard, place the egg yolks and sugar in a bowl and whisk together. Pour the milk into a pan and warm gently over low heat. Remove from the heat and gradually stir into the egg mixture, then return the mixture to the pan and stir constantly over low heat until thickened. Do not boil. Remove from the heat, pour into a heatproof bowl, and stir in the vanilla extract. Let cool for 1 hour. Spread the custard over the trifle, cover with plastic wrap, and let chill for 2 hours.

To make the topping, whip the cream in a bowl and stir in sugar to taste. Spread over the trifle, then sprinkle over the nuts. Cover with plastic wrap and let chill for at least 2 hours before serving.

FESTIVE SHERRY TRIFLE

SERVES 2–4

8 crisp eating apples

1 tbsp lemon juice

½ cup golden raisins

1 tsp ground cinnamon

½ tsp freshly grated nutmeg

1 tbsp brown sugar

6 sheets phyllo pastry

vegetable oil spray

confectioners' sugar, to decorate

Hard cider sauce

1 tbsp cornstarch

2 cups hard cider

Preheat the oven to 375°F/190°C. Line a baking sheet with nonstick liner.

Peel and core the apples and chop them into ½-inch/1-cm dice. Toss the pieces in a bowl with the lemon juice, golden raisins, cinnamon, nutmeg, and brown sugar.

Lay out a sheet of phyllo, spray with vegetable oil, and lay a second sheet on top. Repeat with a third sheet. Spread half the apple mixture over the pastry and roll up lengthwise, tucking in the ends to enclose the filling. Repeat to make a second strudel. Slide onto the baking sheet, spray with oil, and bake in the oven for 15–20 minutes.

To make the sauce, blend the cornstarch in a pan with a little hard cider until smooth. Add the remaining hard cider and heat gently, stirring all the time, until the mixture boils and thickens. Serve the strudel warm or cold, dredged with confectioners' sugar, and accompanied by the hard cider sauce.

APPLE STRUDEL
WITH WARM CIDER SAUCE

Preheat the oven to 350°F/180°C. Brush 4 small tartlet pans with oil.

Cut the phyllo pastry sheets in half to give 16 squares measuring about 4½ inches/12 cm across. Brush each square with oil and use to line the tartlet pans. Place 4 sheets in each pan, staggering them so that the overhanging corners make a decorative star shape. Transfer to a baking sheet and bake in the oven for 7–8 minutes, or until golden. Remove from the oven and set aside.

Meanwhile, place the fruit in a pan with the sugar and allspice over medium heat until simmering. Reduce the heat and continue simmering, stirring, for 10 minutes. Remove from the heat and drain. Using a slotted spoon, divide the warm fruit between the pastry shells. Garnish with mint sprigs and serve warm with cream.

SERVES 4

2–3 tbsp lemon-flavored oil

8 sheets frozen phyllo pastry, thawed

1⅛ cups blueberries

1⅛ cups raspberries

1⅛ cups blackberries

3 tbsp superfine sugar

1 tsp allspice

fresh mint sprigs, to decorate

heavy cream, to serve

WARM FRUIT NESTS

CHOCOLATE WON TONS
WITH MAPLE SAUCE

SERVES 4

16 won ton skins

12 oz/350 g semisweet chocolate, chopped

1 tbsp cornstarch

3 tbsp cold water

4 cups peanut oil

vanilla ice cream, to serve

Maple sauce

3/4 cup maple syrup

4 tbsp butter

1/2 tsp allspice

Spread out the won ton skins on a clean counter, then spoon a little chocolate into the center of each skin. In a small bowl, mix the cornstarch and water together until smooth. Brush the edges of the skins with the cornstarch mixture, then wrap in any preferred shape, such as triangles, squares, or bundles, and seal the edges. Arrange the won tons on a serving platter.

To make the maple sauce, place all the ingredients in a pan and stir over medium heat. Bring to a boil, then reduce the heat and let simmer for 3 minutes.

Meanwhile, pour the oil into a metal fondue pot (it should be no more than one-third full). Heat on the stove to 350–375°F/180–190°C, or until a cube of bread browns in 30 seconds. Using protective gloves, transfer the fondue pot to a lit tabletop burner. To serve, "invite" your guests to place the won tons on metal spoons and dip them into the hot oil until cooked (they will need about 2–3 minutes). Drain off the excess oil. Serve with vanilla ice cream and the sauce.

CHRISTMAS PUNCH

MULLED WINE

SERVES 10

4 cups red wine

4 tbsp sugar

1 cinnamon stick

1¾ cups boiling water

generous ⅓ cup brandy

generous ⅓ cup sherry

generous ⅓ cup orange-flavored liqueur, such as Cointreau

2 unpeeled seedless oranges, cut into wedges

2 unpeeled eating apples, cored and cut into wedges

Place the wine, sugar, and cinnamon stick in a large pan and stir together well. Warm over low heat, stirring, until just starting to simmer, but do not let it boil. Remove from the heat and strain through a strainer. Remove and discard the cinnamon stick.

Return the wine to the pan and stir in the water, brandy, sherry, and liqueur. Add the orange and apple wedges and warm gently over very low heat, but do not let it boil. Remove from the heat and pour into a large, heatproof punch bowl. Ladle into heatproof glasses and serve hot.

CHRISTMAS PUNCH

MULLED WINE

SERVES 4

scant 3 cups red wine

3 tbsp sherry

8 cloves

1 cinnamon stick

½ tsp allspice

2 tbsp honey

1 unpeeled seedless orange, cut
into wedges

1 unpeeled lemon, cut into wedges

Place the wine, sherry, cloves, cinnamon stick, allspice, and honey in a
pan and stir together well. Warm over low heat, stirring, until just starting
to simmer, but do not let it boil. Remove from the heat and strain through
a strainer. Remove and discard the cloves and cinnamon stick.

Return the wine to the pan with the orange and lemon wedges. Warm
gently over very low heat, but do not let it boil. Remove from the heat,
pour into heatproof glasses, and serve hot.

FAST FUN FARE

SMOKED FISH PÂTÉ

SERVES 4

12 oz/350 g smoked mackerel,
skinned and boned

6 oz/175 g butter, melted

½ cup heavy cream

3 tbsp lemon juice

salt and pepper

pinch of cayenne pepper

lemon slice twist, to garnish

Place the fish in a food processor and blend with half the melted butter to a smooth paste.

Transfer the mixture to a bowl and gradually add the remaining butter, along with the cream and lemon juice. Season to taste with salt and pepper.

Spoon into a serving dish and sprinkle with cayenne.

Cover with plastic wrap and let chill for at least 1 hour before serving, garnished with a lemon slice twist.

SERVES 4

2 packages nachos or tortilla chips

4 tbsp bottled sliced jalapeño chilies

1 cup grated Cheddar cheese

2 tbsp finely chopped fresh cilantro, to garnish

To serve
tomato salsa

Guacamole (see page 29)

sour cream

HOT SALSA NACHOS

Preheat the oven to 375°F/190°C.

Tip the nachos into a shallow ovenproof dish. Sprinkle with the chilies and top with the cheese. Bake for 5–10 minutes, or until the cheese has melted.

Remove the nachos from the oven, garnish with cilantro, and serve with salsa, Guacamole, and a dish of sour cream.

½ tsp turmeric

6 skinless, boneless chicken breasts

salt and pepper

4 cups peanut oil

Dippers

4 unsmoked lean bacon slices

cherry tomatoes

whole pearl onions, peeled

white mushrooms

Mustard dip

4 tbsp sour cream

4 tbsp mayonnaise

2 tbsp whole-grain mustard

1 tsp honey

1 scallion, finely chopped

pinch of paprika

To serve

sautéed new potatoes

fresh mixed salad

Rub the turmeric over the chicken, then season to taste with salt and pepper and cut into strips. Stretch the bacon until doubled in length and cut into thin strips lengthwise. Roll up the strips of chicken and bacon and thread them onto wooden skewers with the other dippers, leaving plenty of space at either end. Skewer the tomatoes separately, as they will need less time to cook.

Mix the ingredients for the dip together in a bowl.

Pour the oil into a metal fondue pot (it should be no more than one-third full), then heat on the stove to 350–375°F/180–190°C, or until a cube of bread browns in 30 seconds. Using protective gloves, carefully transfer the fondue pot to a lit tabletop burner.

"Invite" guests to dip the skewers into the fondue, and cook in the hot oil for 2–3 minutes, or until cooked to taste (the chicken and bacon must be cooked right through). Drain off the excess oil, then serve with potatoes, a mixed salad, and the dip.

SKEWERED CHICKEN
WITH MUSTARD DIP

MIDDLE EASTERN KOFTAS

SERVES 4

1 lb 10 oz/750 g fresh ground lamb or beef

1 small onion, quartered

2 garlic cloves, crushed

2 tbsp chopped fresh flat-leaf parsley

1 tsp coriander seeds

$\frac{1}{2}$ tsp cumin seeds

$\frac{1}{2}$ tsp whole black peppercorns

generous pinch of ground cinnamon

pinch of salt

Sesame Seed Sauce (see page 58)

fresh mint sprigs and lemon wedges, to garnish

Serving suggestions

rice or Indian bread

Tzatziki (see page 35)

tomato and onion salad

Blend the meat, onion, garlic, parsley, spices, and salt to a smooth paste in a food processor. Turn into a large bowl.

Select flat skewers that will fit comfortably on your stove-top grill pan.

Take about 2 tablespoons of meat paste and roll gently between your palms to make a sausage shape. Carefully fold around the skewer. If you cannot find flat skewers, shape the meat into patties as you would for hamburgers.

Preheat the stove-top grill pan over high heat. Brush the koftas with the Sesame Seed Sauce and cook for 10 minutes, turning carefully and basting regularly.

When the meat is cooked, transfer to a large serving platter and garnish with mint sprigs and lemon wedges. Serve with rice and bowls of tzatziki and tomato and onion salad.

raw jumbo shrimp in their shells

a little sunflower oil

cherry tomatoes

24 baby corn (optional)

2 tbsp vegetable oil, for basting

fresh flat-leaf parsley sprigs, to garnish

buttered rice, to serve

SEAFOOD BROCHETTES

TUNA & RED CHILI SIZZLERS

GOLDEN
CHEESE MELTS

2 tbsp grated romano cheese

2 eggs

5 tbsp all-purpose flour

6 oz/175 g canned tuna, drained and flaked

1 tbsp grated fresh gingerroot

1 tbsp grated lemon rind

scant 5/8 cup corn kernels

1/2 tsp finely chopped fresh red chili

4 cups peanut oil

fresh mixed salad, to serve

Red chili dipping sauce

1/2 cup plain yogurt

4 tbsp mayonnaise

1 fresh red chili, seeded and finely chopped

1 tbsp lime juice

Dippers

selection of vegetables, cut into bite-size pieces

whole cooked peeled shrimp

Place the cheese, eggs, and flour in a large bowl and beat together. Add the tuna, ginger, lemon rind, corn, and the 1/2 teaspoon of chopped red chili and stir together well.

Meanwhile, to make the sauce, place all the ingredients in a nonmetallic serving bowl, mix together, and set aside. Arrange the dippers on serving plates.

Pour the oil into a metal fondue pot (it should be no more than one-third full), then heat on the stove to 350–375°F/180–190°C, or until a cube of bread browns in 30 seconds. Using protective gloves, carefully transfer the fondue pot to a lit tabletop burner. To serve, "invite" your guests to spear the dippers onto fondue forks and cook them with dessertspoonfuls of the tuna mixture (using heatproof spoons) in the hot oil for about 3 minutes, or until cooked to their taste. Drain off the excess oil, then serve with the dipping sauce and a mixed salad.

TUNA & RED CHILI SIZZLERS

SERVES 4

generous 1¾ cups all-purpose flour

¼ tsp cayenne pepper

14 oz/400 g Edam cheese, rind removed and cut into bite-size cubes

1 tsp baking powder

1 tsp salt

2 large eggs

½ cup milk

4 cups peanut oil

fresh mixed salad, to serve

Dippers

whole white mushrooms

whole cherry tomatoes

blanched broccoli florets

Sift generous 1 cup of the flour with the cayenne into a large bowl. Add the cheese cubes and turn until coated. Shake off the excess flour, then arrange the cheese on a platter. Place the remaining flour in a separate large bowl with the baking powder and salt, then gradually beat in the eggs, milk, and 1 tablespoon of the oil. Beat until the batter is smooth, then pour it into a serving bowl.

Pour the remaining oil into a metal fondue pot (it should be no more than one-third full), then heat on the stove to 350–375°F/180–190°C, or until a cube of bread browns in 30 seconds. Using protective gloves, carefully transfer the fondue pot to a lit tabletop burner. To serve, "invite" your guests to spear the cheese cubes onto fondue forks, dip in the batter, and let the excess run off, then cook in the hot oil for 1 minute, or until golden and crisp. Cook the other dippers in the same way, or leave them without batter and cook to your taste. Drain off the excess oil and serve with a mixed salad.

GOLDEN CHEESE MELTS

SERVES

all-purpose flour, for dusting

2 red onions

2 tbsp olive oil

garlic cloves, chopped

cups canned chopped tomatoes

1 tbsp chopped fresh oregano

1 tsp dried mixed herbs

1 bay leaf

2½ tbsp tomato paste

¼ tsp sugar

2 tsp butter

7 oz/200 g white mushrooms, sliced

2 ready-prepared pizza bases, about 9 inches/23 cm in diameter

10½ oz/300 g mozzarella cheese, chopped

4 tomatoes, sliced

1 red bell pepper, seeded and cut into thin strips

salt and pepper

fresh basil leaves, to garnish

stirring for minutes. Add the chopped tomatoes, oregano, mixed herbs, bay leaf, tomato paste, sugar, and salt and pepper to taste.

stirring for minutes until thickened. Season to taste, adding sugar.

Place a pizza base on each prepared sheet. Spread tomato sauce over each base. Sprinkle over the cheese, remaining garlic, and basil. Arrange the sliced mushrooms, tomatoes, and pepper over the top and drizzle over the remaining oil. Bake for 20–25 minutes. Remove from the oven and garnish with basil.

TOMATO
& MOZZARELLA PIZZAS

SPEEDY CHILI BEEF

SERVES 4

3 tbsp vegetable oil

1 lb/450 g fresh ground beef

1 onion, finely chopped

1 green bell pepper, seeded and diced

2 garlic cloves, very finely chopped

1 lb 12 oz/800 g chopped tomatoes

1½ cups canned red kidney beans,
drained and rinsed

1 tsp ground cumin

1 tsp salt

1 tsp sugar

1–3 tsp chili powder

2 tbsp chopped fresh cilantro

Heat the oil in a large ovenproof casserole over medium–high heat. Add the beef and cook, stirring, until lightly browned.

Reduce the heat to medium. Add the onion, bell pepper, and garlic and cook for 5 minutes, or until soft.

Stir in the remaining ingredients, except the cilantro. Bring to a boil, then let simmer over medium–low heat, stirring frequently, for 30 minutes.

Stir in the cilantro just before serving.

SPANISH MANCHEGO FONDUE

WITH OLIVES

SERVES 4

1 garlic clove, peeled and halved

scant 2 cups Spanish dry
white wine

finely grated rind of 1 lemon or lime

1 lb 9 oz/700 g manchego
cheese, grated

2 tbsp cornstarch

salt and pepper

Dippers

fresh crusty bread, cut into
bite-size pieces

cured chorizo, cut into bite-size
pieces and lightly fried in olive oil

whole green and black olives, pitted

Rub the inside of an ovenproof fondue pot with the garlic. Discard the garlic. Pour in the wine and add the lemon rind, then transfer to the stove and bring to a gentle simmer over low heat. Toss the cheese in the cornstarch, then gradually stir the cheese into the heated liquid and stir constantly until melted. Continue to add the cheese gradually, stirring constantly, until all the cheese has melted and the liquid is bubbling gently. Stir until thick and creamy. Season to taste with salt and pepper.

Using protective gloves, transfer the fondue pot to a lit tabletop burner. To serve, "invite" your guests to spear bread, chorizo, and olives onto fondue forks and dip them into the fondue.

PESTO
FONDUE

SERVES 4

1¼ oz/35 g fresh basil,
finely chopped

3 garlic cloves, finely chopped

10½ oz/300 g fontina cheese,
chopped

1⅛ cups ricotta cheese

½ cup freshly grated Parmesan
cheese

2 tbsp lemon juice

scant 1¾ cups vegetable stock

1 tbsp cornstarch

salt and pepper

Dippers

fresh Italian bread, such as
ciabatta or focaccia, cut into
bite-size pieces

selection of lightly cooked
vegetables, cut into
bite-size pieces

Place the basil and garlic in a large bowl. Add all the cheeses and stir together well. Place the lemon juice and all but 2 tablespoons of the stock in a large pan and bring to a gentle simmer over low heat. Add a small spoonful of the cheese mixture and stir constantly until melted. Continue to add the cheese mixture gradually, stirring constantly after each addition. Repeat until all the cheese mixture has been added and stir until thoroughly melted and bubbling gently. Mix the cornstarch with the remaining stock, then stir into the pan. Continue to stir for 3–4 minutes, or until thickened and bubbling. Season to taste with salt and pepper.

Pour the mixture into a fondue pot and, using protective gloves, transfer to a lit tabletop burner. To serve, "invite" your guests to spear pieces of bread and vegetables onto fondue forks and dip them into the fondue.

SERVES 4

1 lb/450 g boneless pork, cubed

Sweet-&-Sour Marinade
(see page 65)

2 carrots, thickly sliced

1 small red bell pepper,
seeded and quartered

1 small green bell pepper,
seeded and quartered

2 tomatoes, halved

1 onion, quartered

Mix the pork with the marinade in a nonmetallic bowl. Cover with plastic wrap and let chill for 1 hour, stirring occasionally. Blanch the carrots for 5 minutes in a pan of boiling water. Drain and let cool.

Remove the meat from the refrigerator and stir. Drain from the marinade. Preheat a stove-top grill pan over medium heat. Thread the meat and vegetables onto skewers that will fit comfortably on the grill pan. Cook the kabobs on the grill pan, turning frequently, for 10–15 minutes, or until the meat is cooked right through and tender.

To make the sauce, mix the cornstarch and sugar together in a small pan. Add the vinegar and sherry, stirring to eliminate lumps. Gradually add the water and tomato paste, still stirring. Mix in the ginger pieces and syrup. Cook over medium heat, stirring constantly, until it comes to the boil and thickens slightly.

Serve the kabobs drizzled with a spoonful of the sauce.

SWEET & SOUR PORK KABOBS

Sauce

2 tbsp cornstarch

2 tsp sugar

1 tbsp wine vinegar

2 tbsp sweet sherry

2$\frac{1}{2}$ cups water

3 tbsp tomato paste

8 pieces preserved ginger, diced

2 tbsp ginger syrup

SERVES 4

4 cherry or baby plum tomatoes

2 zucchini, halved and sliced
into chunks

8 white mushrooms

4 whole shallots, peeled

2 red or green bell peppers,
seeded and quartered

4 tbsp olive oil

salt and pepper

2 tbsp chopped fresh basil
or oregano, to garnish

fresh salad greens, to serve

VEGETABLE KABOBS

Preheat a stove-top grill pan over high heat.

Meanwhile, arrange all the vegetables on skewers
that will fit comfortably on the grill pan, alternating
to create a colorful selection. Brush with oil and
season to taste with salt and pepper.

Cook the kabobs on the grill pan, turning frequently,
for 10 minutes. Baste with oil occasionally so that the
vegetables do not dry out.

Remove the kabobs from the grill pan, arrange
on a serving platter, garnish with chopped herbs,
and serve with salad greens.

SERVES 4

scant 1¾ cups packed brown sugar

½ cup water

1 tbsp rum

6 tbsp unsalted butter

½ cup heavy cream, gently warmed

scant ⅔ cup peanuts, chopped

Dippers

popcorn

firm ripe bananas, cut into bite-size pieces

sliced apples

Arrange the dippers decoratively on a serving platter or individual serving plates and set aside.

Place the sugar and water in a heavy-bottom pan over medium heat and stir until the sugar has dissolved. Bring to a boil, then let bubble for 6–7 minutes. Stir in the rum and cook for an additional minute.

Using protective gloves, remove from the heat and carefully stir in the butter until melted. Gradually stir in the cream until the mixture is smooth. Finally, stir in the chopped nuts.

Carefully pour the mixture into a warmed fondue pot, then transfer to a lit tabletop burner. To serve, "invite" your guests to spear the dippers onto fondue forks and dip them into the fondue.

BUTTERSCOTCH FONDUE
WITH POPCORN

BANANA SPLITS

SERVES 4

4 bananas

**6 tbsp chopped mixed nuts,
to decorate**

Vanilla ice cream

1¼ cups milk

1 tsp vanilla extract

3 egg yolks

½ cup superfine sugar

1¼ cups heavy cream, whipped

Chocolate rum sauce

**4½ oz/125 g semisweet chocolate,
broken into small pieces**

2½ tbsp butter

6 tbsp water

1 tbsp rum

To make the ice cream, heat the milk and vanilla extract in a pan until almost boiling. In a bowl, beat the egg yolks and sugar together. Remove the milk from the heat and stir a little into the egg mixture. Transfer the mixture to the pan and stir over low heat until thick. Do not boil. Remove from the heat and let cool for 30 minutes. Fold in the cream, cover with plastic wrap, and let chill for 1 hour.

Transfer to an ice-cream maker and process for 15 minutes. Alternatively, transfer to a freezerproof container and freeze for 1 hour, then turn out into a bowl and beat to break up the ice crystals. Return to the container and freeze for 30 minutes. Repeat twice more, freezing for 30 minutes and beating each time.

To make the sauce, melt the chocolate and butter with the water in a pan, stirring. Remove from the heat and stir in the rum. Peel the bananas, slice lengthwise, and arrange on 4 serving dishes. Top with the ice cream and nuts and serve with the sauce.

Peel and core the pineapple. Cut into thick slices, about 1 inch/2.5 cm wide.

Preheat a stove-top grill pan over medium heat. Meanwhile, heat the honey in a small pan over medium heat, or in the microwave, until it is liquid.

Brush both sides of the pineapple slices with the melted butter. Cook on the grill pan for 2 minutes on each side, brushing with the honey before and after turning so that both sides are well coated and sticky.

Remove the hot pineapple from the grill pan. Decorate with mint leaves and serve with a scoop of fruit sherbet, sour cream, whipped cream, or ice cream.

GLAZED PINEAPPLE SLICES

SERVES 4

1 pineapple

¼ cup honey

4 oz/115 g butter, melted

fresh mint leaves, to decorate

Serving suggestions
fruit sherbet

sour cream

whipped cream

ice cream

1½ cups no-soak
dried apricots

1 tbsp honey

scant 1¼ cups freshly squeezed
orange juice

scant 1¼ cups lowfat
plain yogurt

2 tsp slivered almonds, toasted,
to decorate

Place all the ingredients, except the almonds,
in a food processor and blend until smooth.

Serve in individual glass dishes, decorated
with toasted almonds.

APRICOT &
ORANGE FOOL

5
SUPER SUPPER PARTIES

BAKED MEDITERRANEAN VEGETABLES WITH FETA

SERVES 4

1 red onion, sliced into thick rings

1 small eggplant, thickly sliced

2 large mushrooms, halved

3 red bell peppers,
halved and seeded

3 tbsp olive oil, plus extra
for brushing

3 plum tomatoes,
peeled and diced

2 garlic cloves, minced

1 tbsp chopped fresh
flat-leaf parsley

1 tsp chopped fresh rosemary

1 tsp dried thyme or oregano

finely grated rind of 1 lemon

scant ¾ cup stale,
coarse bread crumbs

6–8 black olives, pitted and sliced

1 oz/25 g feta cheese
(drained weight), cut into
½-inch/1-cm cubes

salt and pepper

Preheat the broiler to medium. Place the onion, eggplant, mushrooms, and bell peppers on a large baking sheet, placing the bell peppers cut-side down. Brush lightly with oil.

Cook under the broiler for 10–12 minutes, turning the onion, eggplant, and mushroom halfway through, until starting to blacken. Cut into oven-size chunks. Place in a shallow ovenproof dish. Arrange the diced tomatoes on top. Season to taste with salt and pepper.

Preheat the oven to 425°F/220°C.

In a bowl, combine the garlic, parsley, rosemary, thyme, and lemon rind with the bread crumbs. Season to taste with pepper. Add the 3 tablespoons of oil to bind the mixture together. Sprinkle the mixture over the vegetables. Scatter the olives and cheese over.

Bake in the oven for 10–15 minutes, or until the vegetables are heated through and the topping is crisp. Serve straight from the dish.

6 tbsp mayonnaise

2 garlic cloves, crushed

2 large white fish fillets, skinned

1 egg, beaten

3 heaping tbsp all-purpose flour

vegetable oil, for deep-frying

lemon wedges, to garnish

Combine the mayonnaise and garlic in a small dish. Cover with plastic wrap and let chill while you cook the fish.

Cut the fish into 1-inch/2.5-cm strips. Dip the strips in the egg, then drain and dredge in flour.

Meanwhile, heat the oil in a deep-fryer or large pan to 350–375°F/180–190°C, or until a cube of bread browns in 30 seconds. Fry the pieces of fish in the hot oil for 3–4 minutes, or until golden brown. Remove from the oil and drain on a dish lined with paper towels.

Remove the garlic mayonnaise from the refrigerator and stir once. Serve the fish on an attractive dish, garnished with lemon wedges, with the mayonnaise on the side for dipping.

GOUJONS
WITH GARLIC MAYONNAISE

THAI FISH CAKES

SERVES 4

1 lb 2 oz/500 g skinless, boneless cod fillet, cut into chunks

1 tbsp red curry paste

1 egg, beaten

1 tsp brown sugar

1 tsp salt

1 tbsp cornstarch

¼ cup finely chopped green beans

1 tbsp chopped fresh cilantro

4 tbsp oil, for pan-frying

lime wedges, to garnish

Serving suggestions

fresh salad

stir-fried bean sprouts and green vegetables, such as green beans, snow peas, or broccoli florets

Place the cod in a food processor and coarsely chop. Add the curry paste, egg, sugar, salt, and cornstarch. Blend well.

Stir in the green beans and cilantro.

Transfer to a bowl, cover with plastic wrap, and let chill for 30 minutes. Remove from the refrigerator and roll the mixture into 12 balls, then flatten each ball into a 2-inch/5-cm cake.

Heat the oil in a skillet over medium heat and cook the cakes, in batches, for 3 minutes on each side, or until golden brown and cooked through. Keep the cooked fish cakes warm in a low oven while pan-frying the remainder.

Garnish with lime wedges and serve with salad or stir-fried bean sprouts and green vegetables.

ASIAN PORK CURRY

SERVES 4

2 tbsp chili-flavored oil

1 lb 2 oz/500 g lean pork, cut into bite-size chunks

2 fresh red chilies, chopped

3 scallions, sliced

2 tbsp finely chopped fresh lemon grass

1 tbsp grated fresh gingerroot

1 tbsp curry paste

2 tbsp yellow bean sauce

1 tbsp Thai fish sauce

2 tsp soy sauce

2 tsp sugar

scant 2½ cups coconut milk

1 large potato, cut into bite-size chunks

scant 5/8 cup unsalted peanuts, toasted and crushed

shredded scallion, to garnish

freshly cooked jasmine rice, to serve

Heat half the oil in a preheated wok or large skillet over high heat, add the pork, and cook, stirring, for 5 minutes. Lift out the meat with a slotted spoon and drain on paper towels. Heat the remaining oil in the skillet, add the chilies, scallions, lemon grass, and ginger and cook, stirring, for 4 minutes. Add the curry paste, yellow bean, fish and soy sauces, and sugar and stir well. Add the meat and coconut milk and bring to a boil. Reduce the heat, cover, and let simmer for 40 minutes.

Add the potato, cover, and cook for an additional 20 minutes.

Stir in the crushed peanuts and cook for an additional 5 minutes.

Garnish with shredded scallion and serve with jasmine rice.

SERVES 4

1 lb/450 g skinless,
boneless chicken breasts,
cut into bite-size chunks

1 tsp salt

5 tbsp lemon juice

4–6 tbsp light cream

fresh cilantro sprigs, to garnish

lemon wedges, to serve

Marinade

1 large garlic clove, finely chopped

½ onion, grated

1 tbsp dry unsweetened coconut

1 tsp ground cumin

1½ tsp chili powder

1 tsp garam masala

1 tsp turmeric

1 tsp paprika

1 tsp ground coriander

2 tsp chopped fresh cilantro

generous ⅓ cup plain yogurt

pepper, to taste

CHICKEN TIKKA

Place the chicken, salt, and lemon juice in a nonmetallic bowl and mix together well. In a separate bowl, mix all the marinade ingredients together, then add to the chicken and stir gently to combine. Cover with plastic wrap and let chill for at least 2 hours, or preferably overnight.

When ready to cook, remove from the refrigerator. Thread the chicken onto skewers (presoaked in water for 30 minutes if wooden or bamboo) and baste with the marinade. Barbecue over hot coals or cook under a preheated hot broiler for 15 minutes, turning and basting frequently with remaining marinade.

Remove the chicken skewers from the heat, transfer to a serving platter, and pour over the cream. Garnish with cilantro sprigs and serve with lemon wedges.

Spray a large nonstick skillet with oil. Add the onion and cook, stirring, for 5 minutes, or until softened and lightly colored.

Add the mushrooms and mustard to the skillet and cook, stirring occasionally, for an additional 4–5 minutes, or until lightly colored.

Add the beef to the skillet and cook, stirring occasionally, for 5 minutes, or until tender. Add the sour cream and salt and pepper to taste, then heat, stirring all the time, until hot.

Serve garnished with chopped parsley.

SERVES 4

vegetable oil spray

1 onion, coarsely sliced

8 oz/225 g white mushrooms, thinly sliced

1 tsp French mustard

1 lb/450 g rump or sirloin steak, thinly sliced

1¼ cups reduced-fat sour cream

salt and pepper

chopped fresh parsley, to garnish

BŒUF STROGANOFF

BAKED CHICKEN IN RED WINE

SERVES 4

3 tbsp olive oil

2 garlic cloves, chopped

4 tomatoes,
seeded and chopped

1 tbsp tomato paste

2 tbsp sherry vinegar

6 tbsp red wine

12 black olives, pitted and halved

1 tbsp capers, rinsed and drained

2 tbsp chopped fresh basil

1 tsp dried mixed herbs

4 skinless, boneless
chicken breasts

salt and pepper

fresh basil sprigs, to garnish

fresh crusty bread, to serve

Preheat the oven to 350°F/180°C.

Heat the oil in a pan over low heat. Add the garlic and cook, stirring, for 4 minutes, or until slightly softened.

Add the tomatoes, tomato paste, vinegar, wine, olives, capers, and herbs. Season to taste with salt and pepper. Bring to a boil, then reduce the heat, cover, and let simmer for 10 minutes.

Arrange the chicken in the bottom of an ovenproof baking dish. Remove the tomato sauce from the heat and pour it over the chicken. Bake in the oven for 45 minutes, basting the chicken with the sauce from time to time.

Remove from the oven. Divide the chicken between individual serving plates and pour the sauce over the top, then garnish with basil sprigs and serve with crusty bread.

8 wheat flour tortillas

vegetable oil spray

1 onion, finely chopped

4 skinless, boneless chicken breasts, thinly sliced

1 package taco seasoning

4 tomatoes, coarsely chopped

4 scallions, finely sliced

1 tub tomato salsa, to serve

MEXICAN CHICKEN BURRITOS

Preheat the oven to 300°F/150°C.

Wrap the tortillas in foil and heat in the oven for 10 minutes, or until soft.

Meanwhile, spray a large nonstick skillet with oil. Add the onion and cook for 5 minutes, or until softened. Add the chicken and cook, stirring occasionally, for 5 minutes, or until cooked right through and tender. Stir in the taco seasoning.

Remove the tortillas from the oven and increase the oven temperature to 350°F/180°C. Place an equal quantity of the chicken mixture in the center of each tortilla and add the tomatoes and scallions. Fold each tortilla into a package and place in an ovenproof dish.

Cover the dish and cook in the oven for 20 minutes. Spoon the tomato salsa over the hot tortillas before serving.

Soak the mussels in a bowl of lightly salted water for 10 minutes. Scrub under cold running water and pull out any beards. Discard any with broken shells. Tap the remaining mussels and discard any that refuse to close.

Heat the oil in a large pan over medium heat. Add the garlic and cook, stirring, for 3 minutes. Stir in the wine, water, lemon juice and rind, and herbs. Season to taste with salt and pepper. Bring to a boil, then reduce the heat and let simmer for 5 minutes.

Add the mussels, cover, and let simmer for 5–7 minutes, or until they have opened. Drain, then remove and discard the bay leaf and any mussels that remain closed. Transfer the mussels to a large serving platter or individual serving plates, sprinkle over some parsley and lemon wedges, and serve in their shells with some crusty bread.

You can eat these mussels in the traditional Spanish way, if you wish, by using one half of a mussel shell as a spoon.

SERVES 4

4 lb/1.8 kg live mussels

generous ⅓ cup olive oil

6 garlic cloves, finely chopped

scant 1¼ cups dry white wine

scant 2½ cups water

juice of 1 lemon

1 tbsp finely grated lemon rind

1 bay leaf

3 tbsp chopped fresh flat-leaf parsley, plus extra to garnish

salt and pepper

lemon wedges, to garnish

fresh crusty bread, to serve

SPANISH GARLIC MUSSELS

ROASTED SALMON
WITH LEMON & HERBS

SERVES 4

6 tbsp extra virgin olive oil

1 onion, sliced

1 leek, sliced

juice of ½ lemon

2 tbsp chopped fresh parsley

2 tbsp chopped fresh dill

1 lb 2 oz/500 g salmon fillets

salt and pepper

freshly cooked baby spinach
leaves, to serve

To garnish

lemon slices

fresh dill sprigs

Preheat the oven to 400°F/200°C.

Heat 1 tablespoon of the oil in a skillet over medium heat. Add the onion and leek and cook, stirring, for 4 minutes, or until slightly softened.

Meanwhile, place the remaining oil in a small bowl with the lemon juice and herbs and season to taste with salt and pepper. Stir together well. Rinse the fish under cold running water, then pat dry with paper towels. Arrange the fish in a shallow ovenproof baking dish.

Remove the skillet from the heat and spread the onion and leek over the fish. Pour the oil mixture over the top, ensuring that everything is well coated. Roast in the center of the oven for 10 minutes, or until the fish is cooked through.

Arrange the cooked spinach on serving plates. Remove the fish and vegetables from the oven and arrange on top of the spinach. Garnish with lemon slices and dill sprigs and serve at once.

SERVES 4

8 oz/225 g canned
artichoke hearts

about 8 cups stock
or water

1 tbsp olive oil

3 tbsp butter

1 small onion, finely chopped

1 lb/450 g risotto rice

½ cup freshly grated Parmesan
cheese or Grana Padano

salt and pepper

Drain the artichoke hearts, adding the liquid to the stock to give a total volume of 8½ cups. Cut the artichoke hearts into quarters and set aside.

Bring the stock to a boil in a pan, then reduce the heat and keep simmering gently on low heat while you are cooking the risotto.

Heat the oil with 2 tablespoons of the butter in a deep pan over medium heat until the butter has melted. Add the onion and cook gently, stirring frequently, until soft and starting to turn golden. Do not brown.

Add the rice and mix to coat in the oil and butter. Cook, stirring, for 2–3 minutes, or until the grains are translucent. Gradually add the stock, a ladleful at a time, stirring constantly and adding more liquid as the rice absorbs it. Increase the heat to medium so that the liquid bubbles. Cook for 15 minutes, then add the artichoke hearts. Cook for an additional 5 minutes, or until all the liquid is absorbed. Season to taste with salt and pepper but don't add too much salt as the Parmesan cheese is salty. The finished risotto should be of a creamy consistency with a little "bite" in the rice.

Remove the risotto from the heat and stir in the remaining butter. Mix well, then add the Parmesan cheese and stir until it melts. Check and adjust the seasoning, then serve.

RISOTTO WITH ARTICHOKE HEARTS

SERVES 4

1 lb/450 g frozen spinach, thawed

1 lb/450 g ricotta cheese

8 sheets no-precook lasagna

scant 2½ cups strained tomatoes

8 oz/225 g mozzarella cheese, thinly sliced

1 tbsp freshly grated Parmesan cheese

salt and pepper

fresh salad, to serve (optional)

Preheat the oven to 350°F/180°C.

Place the spinach in a strainer and squeeze out any excess liquid. Place half in the bottom of an ovenproof dish and add salt and pepper to taste.

Spread half the ricotta over the spinach, cover with half the lasagna sheets, then spoon over half the strained tomatoes. Arrange half the mozzarella slices on top. Repeat the layers and finally sprinkle over the Parmesan cheese.

Bake in the oven for 45–50 minutes, or until the top is brown and bubbling.

Serve with salad, if desired.

CHEESE & SPINACH LASAGNA

MOCHA FONDUE

SERVES 4

9 oz/250 g semisweet chocolate (must contain at least 50 percent cocoa solids)

generous 1/3 cup heavy cream

1 tbsp instant coffee powder

3 tbsp coffee-flavored liqueur, such as Kahlúa

Dippers

sweet cookies, such as amaretti

plain or coffee-flavored marbled cake or sponge cake, cut into bite-size pieces

whole seedless grapes

sliced firm peaches or nectarines

Arrange the dippers decoratively on a serving platter or individual serving plates and set aside.

Break or chop the chocolate into small pieces and place in the top of a double boiler or in a heatproof bowl set over a pan of barely simmering water. Add the cream and coffee powder and stir until melted and smooth. Stir in the liqueur, then carefully pour the mixture into a warmed fondue pot.

Using protective gloves, transfer the fondue pot to a lit tabletop burner. To serve, "invite" your guests to spear the dippers onto fondue forks and dip them into the fondue.

ORANGE SHERBET

BAKED PEACHES
WITH ORANGE LIQUEUR CREAM

ORANGE SHERBET

SERVES 4

scant 2½ cups water

1 cup superfine sugar

4 large oranges

2 tbsp orange-flavored liqueur, such as Cointreau

4 scooped-out oranges, to serve

Heat the water and sugar in a pan over low heat, stirring, until dissolved. Boil without stirring for 2 minutes. Pour into a heatproof bowl. Let cool to room temperature.

Meanwhile, grate the rind from 2 of the oranges and extract the juice. Extract the juice from the remaining oranges. Mix the juice and rind together in a bowl, cover with plastic wrap, and set aside.

Stir the orange juice, grated rind, and liqueur into the cooled syrup. Cover with plastic wrap and let chill for 1 hour. Transfer to an ice-cream maker and process for 15 minutes. Alternatively, transfer to a freezerproof container and freeze for 1 hour, then turn out into a bowl and beat to break up the ice crystals. Return to the container and freeze for 30 minutes. Repeat twice more, freezing for 30 minutes and beating each time.

Divide the sherbet between the scooped-out orange cups and serve at once.

SERVES 4

generous 3/8 cup shelled pistachios, finely chopped

generous 3/8 cup toasted hazelnuts, finely chopped

1 tbsp grated orange rind

1 tbsp brown sugar

pinch of allspice

4 large, ripe (but firm) peaches

1 tbsp unsalted butter

Honey syrup

1/2 cup water

1 tbsp honey

2 tsp freshly squeezed orange juice

generous 3/4 cup superfine sugar

pinch of allspice

Orange liqueur cream

1 tbsp finely grated orange rind

1/2 cup heavy cream

1 tbsp orange-flavored liqueur, such as Cointreau

Preheat the oven to 350°F/180°C.

Place the nuts, orange rind, brown sugar, and allspice in a bowl and stir together well. Halve and pit the peaches. Remove a little of the flesh in the center of each peach, chop into pieces, and stir into the nut mixture. Place a little of the mixture into the hollow of each peach. Transfer the peaches to an ovenproof dish and dot with butter. Bake in the oven for 30 minutes.

About halfway through the cooking time, make the honey syrup. Place the water, honey, orange juice, superfine sugar, and allspice in a pan and bring to a boil, stirring constantly. Reduce the heat and let simmer, without stirring, for 15 minutes.

To make the orange liqueur cream, place the orange rind and cream in a bowl and beat together, then stir in the liqueur. Remove the peaches from the oven and divide between serving dishes. Pour over the honey syrup and serve with the orange liqueur cream.

BAKED PEACHES
WITH ORANGE LIQUEUR CREAM

MIXED FRUIT PAVLOVA

SERVES 4

6 egg whites

pinch of cream of tartar

pinch of salt

1³/₈ cups superfine sugar

2¹/₂ cups heavy cream

1 tsp vanilla extract

2 kiwifruit, sliced

**9 oz/250 g strawberries,
hulled and sliced**

3 ripe peaches, sliced

1 ripe mango, sliced

**2 tbsp orange-flavored liqueur,
such as Cointreau**

fresh mint leaves, to decorate

Preheat the oven to 225°F/110°C. Line 3 baking sheets with parchment paper, then draw an 8¹/₂-inch/22-cm circle in the center of each one.

Beat the egg whites in a large bowl into stiff peaks. Mix in the cream of tartar and salt. Gradually add 1 cup of the sugar. Beat for 2 minutes until glossy. Fill a pastry bag with the meringue mixture and pipe enough to fill each circle, doming them slightly in the center. Bake in the oven for 3 hours. Remove from the oven and let cool.

Whip the cream, vanilla extract, and the remaining sugar together in a bowl. Place the fruit in a separate bowl and stir in the liqueur. Place one meringue circle on a serving plate, then spread over one-third of the sugared cream. Spread over one-third of the fruit, then top with a meringue circle. Spread over another third of cream, then another third of fruit. Top with the last meringue circle. Spread over the remaining cream, followed by the remaining fruit. Decorate with mint leaves and serve.

GOLDEN BAKED APPLE PUDDING

SERVES 4

1 lb/450 g cooking apples

1 tsp ground cinnamon

2 tbsp golden raisins

4 oz/115 g whole-wheat bread

generous ½ cup lowfat cottage cheese

4 tbsp brown sugar

scant 1¼ cups semiskim milk

Preheat the oven to 425°F/220°C.

Peel and core the apples and chop the flesh into ½-inch/1-cm pieces. Place in a bowl and toss with the cinnamon and golden raisins.

Remove the crusts and cut the bread into ½-inch/1-cm cubes. Add to the apples with the cottage cheese and 3 tablespoons of the sugar and mix together. Stir in the milk.

Turn the mixture into an ovenproof dish and sprinkle with the remaining sugar. Bake in the oven for 30–35 minutes, or until golden brown. Serve hot.

Reserving a few whole raspberries to decorate, use the back of a spoon to push the raspberries and cottage cheese through a nylon strainer into a bowl.

Stir the sugar and yogurt into the raspberry mixture and stir to blend, then spoon into individual serving dishes. Cover and let chill for about 1 hour.

Serve chilled, decorated with the reserved raspberries, and dusted with sifted confectioners' sugar.

SERVES 4

1 lb/450 g fresh raspberries

³⁄₄ cup lowfat cottage cheese

3 tbsp sugar

**²⁄₃ cup lowfat
plain yogurt**

confectioners' sugar, to decorate

RASPBERRY
CREAMS

CHERRY PUDDINGS

MOCHA CREAM

SERVES 2

scant 1 cup milk

¼ cup light cream

1 tbsp brown sugar

2 tbsp unsweetened cocoa

1 tbsp coffee syrup or instant
coffee powder

6 ice cubes

To decorate

whipped cream

grated chocolate

Place the milk, cream, and sugar in a food processor and process gently until combined.

Add the unsweetened cocoa and coffee syrup and process well, then add the ice cubes and process until smooth.

Pour the mixture into glasses. Top with whipped cream, sprinkle over the grated chocolate, and serve.

INDEX